WORDS OF
TRAINING
FOR THE NEW WAY

Witness Lee

V O L U M E   O N E

Living Stream Ministry
Anaheim, California

First Edition, 6,250 copies. December 1988.

ISBN 0-87083-406-1 (hardcover)
ISBN 0-87083-407-X (softcover)

Published by

Living Stream Ministry
1853 W. Ball Road, Anaheim, CA 92804 U.S.A.
P. O. Box 2121, Anaheim, CA 92814 U.S.A.

Printed in the United States of America

CONTENTS

CONTENTS

PREFACE

This volume is a translation from the Chinese of messages given in Taipei, Taiwan, by Brother Witness Lee in 1987. The first message was given in a conference in April. The second and third messages were given to the serving ones in the Living Stream Ministry office in April and May. The remaining nine messages were given during the months of August through October to trainees participating in the Full-time Training in Taipei, Taiwan.

CHAPTER ONE

THE ADMINISTRATION OF GOD'S NEW TESTAMENT ECONOMY

Scripture Reading: Matt. 16:16-18; Eph. 4:11-13

The administration of God's New Testament economy is simply the move of God on the earth today. In the New Testament not only does God reveal to us His New Testament economy, but He also shows us step by step the administration of that economy by means of both clear words and patterns of practice.

CONFUSION DUE TO THE DEGRADATION OF THE CHURCH

Unfortunately, due to the degradation of the church in the last two thousand years, the church followed after man's desires and became mixed with the world so that the clear revelation and pattern of the administration of God's New Testament economy became completely obscured. We were born with such a background of confusion and were also affected by the confusing situation and atmosphere of Christianity. Although the Lord brought us into His recovery over sixty years ago, it has not been easy for us to be freed from this kind of confusing situation. The practices in Christianity with its confusion fit in with the worldly taste and with man's natural inclination. Therefore, after a person believes in the Lord and becomes a Christian, without any special effort he spontaneously comes under that atmosphere and inclination and is unable to be freed from the confusing situation of Christianity.

For more than sixty years, our burden has been the matter of Christ and the church in God's economy. We have published many messages concerning the great mystery of Christ and the church. However, every time we testify for God according to this mystery, there is a big conflict between us and Christianity over the matter of the church practice, that is, the matter of the administration of God's New Testament economy. The opposition, resistance, and slandering have risen up from this point. All the weaknesses among us are also due to the confusions and mistakes in the church practice. These confusions and mistakes have suppressed and even killed the spiritual life of many saints. They have also hindered and weakened the increase and spread of the church so that the church has been in a half-dormant condition.

I hope that all the brothers and sisters can put aside their backgrounds and circumstances, and all the influences they have been under as well. We need to come together to the pure Word of God to see what is the administration of God's New Testament economy.

FOR THE BUILDING UP OF THE CHURCH

The New Testament shows us that the purpose of the Lord in saving sinners is to obtain a builded church. In Matthew 16:16, after Peter received the revelation from the Father to recognize Jesus as the Christ, the Son of the living God, the Lord Jesus spoke to him, saying, "And I also say to you...on this rock I will build My church" (v. 18). The Lord Jesus shows us here that it is not enough to know Him as the Christ and the Son of the living God, but we also need to know the church which He will build "on this rock." This rock does not merely refer to Christ, but it also refers to the revelation concerning Christ. Christ will build the church according to this revelation.

In Acts the Lord Jesus had gained a group of followers among whom were apostles, prophets, evangelists, and shepherds and teachers (Eph. 4:11). They were raised up by Christ, produced through the death and resurrection of Christ, and appointed by Christ in the Holy Spirit. Christ gave these persons as gifts to the church for its building up. These were the ones who preached the gospel on the earth and brought people to be saved that they might receive the life of God. They also taught them the truth that they might know God, His heart's desire, His plan, His purpose, and all the spiritual matters which are related to God's New Testament economy. Then in each locality they built up this group of believers who had been saved and nurtured in the truth. On the one hand, as to the universal aspect, this group of believers is the one Body of Christ, which is God's unique church on the earth. On the other hand, this unique church is expressed through groups of believers in many localities. The churches which are expressed in each locality are the local churches. The number of localities determines the number of local churches. Therefore, regarding the church, there are two aspects, the universal aspect and the local aspect. The universal church is mysterious and abstract; hence, it is relatively simple. But the local church is manifest and exists before our eyes. None of us who are in the church can be separated from the local church. Therefore, there must be God's administration in the local churches.

THE PROPER ADMINISTRATION OF GOD'S NEW TESTAMENT ECONOMY

The Relationship between the Apostles and the Local Churches

After the apostles establish a local church, they appoint elders to take care of the church and to take the lead, and appoint deacons to serve and to handle business affairs in the church as well. At the same time, they teach the saints to function in the meetings and to preach the gospel fervently outside the meetings. Up to now, we can see that there is the universal church, and there are the local churches; there are the apostles, the prophets, the evangelists, and the shepherds and teachers, and there are the local elders, deacons, and functioning ones. Now we come to consider the relationship between the apostles and the local churches. The apostles have their work, and the local churches have their respective administrations, management, service relating to business affairs, and various functions. What should the relationship be between these two? We need to see the proper administration of

God's New Testament economy from the revelation in the Bible.

The Apostles and Their Work
Being the Source of the Local Churches

First, the Bible shows us that the local churches are produced by the work of the apostles. The apostles and their work are the source of the local churches. Therefore, in the New Testament the apostles always have the ground to speak to and teach the church in a given locality.

Each Local Church Being Independent,
Not under the Direct Oversight of the Apostles

The Bible also shows us that once the apostles have established a local church, they then turn it over to the elders for them to oversee and take the lead, to the deacons for them to serve and handle business affairs, and to all the saints for them to function and to preach the gospel to save sinners. Therefore, every local church is independent. Not one church is in the hands of the apostles nor under their direct oversight, but every church is in the hands of the local elders, deacons, and all the saints. If they all would walk according to the teaching of the apostles, then the apostles would need to help them only in the positive aspects. If the behavior or actions of a local church have deviated from the truth, if there are sinful situations or confusion, then the apostles have the ground to step in to speak to them and correct them.

The Example of the Church in Corinth

Such a relationship was clearly illustrated in the church in Corinth. It must have been that, after the apostle had preached the gospel, taught the truth, and established the church, he also appointed elders and deacons and handed the church over completely to the local elders, deacons, and all the saints. But not long after Paul left, there were problems including divisions, fornication, and idolatry in the church in Corinth. Then the Apostle Paul had to speak to them, teaching and even warning them, saying, "Shall I come to you with a rod...?" (1 Cor. 4:21). This strongly proves that after the apostle had handed the church over to the local elders, deacons, and all the saints, he still had the ground to speak and teach, yet not in the way of direct oversight. When there was someone in the church in Corinth who committed fornication, the apostle said, "Remove the evil man from among yourselves" (1 Cor. 5:13). He did not say to wait for him to come so that he could remove that person himself. He did not have the position to exercise oversight directly, but he had the position to teach them. There is a difference. It does not mean that the apostles cannot intervene in the matters of the local church, nor does it mean that they exercise direct oversight in the matters of the local church.

The Proof in 1 Timothy 5

In 1 Timothy 5:19-20 the Apostle Paul charged Timothy, saying, "Against an elder do not receive an accusation, except on the word of two or three witnesses. Those who sin [referring to the accused elders who have sinned] reprove before all [referring to the church] that the rest also may be in fear." Timothy was an apostle (1 Thes. 1:1; 2:6) and was also a representative of the Apostle Paul. Regarding the matter of eldership, Paul's charge to Timothy indicates the following two points: First, after the apostles had handed the church over to the elders appointed by them for their care, if the elders did not conduct themselves properly, the apostles still had the position to intervene, even to judge. Second, the apostles had the position to reprove the elders who had sinned. This shows the authority of the apostles in relation to the elders. The elders are to submit themselves to the authority of the apostles. This is concerning dealings on the negative side.

On the positive side, the apostles visit the local churches established by them again and again to strengthen them, to instruct them, and to enlighten them that they may know how a local church should conduct itself in order to accomplish God's purpose on the earth today. This is the proper relationship between the apostles and the churches.

The Relationship between the Apostles and Those Who Serve and Supply Them in Their Work

According to the Bible we see also that the apostles are corporate, not individual. When the Lord Jesus first appointed apostles, He appointed twelve at the same time. In the book of Acts the apostles moved and worked as a corporate body, not as individuals. Not only so, because there is so much to the Lord's work that it is beyond what a few can handle, God has sovereignly arranged some to be one with the apostles to serve them and their work.

The Picture in the Old Testament

In the Old Testament God appointed priests to serve Him. The priesthood was a group of people, not individuals. Their service involved many items, such as killing the oxen, slaying the lambs, offering sacrifices, sprinkling the blood, caring for the temple, lighting the lamps, burning the incense, preparing the showbread, and collecting the offerings from the people. For this reason, besides the priests God prepared a group of Levites to minister to the priests and to their services. This is a clear picture in the Old Testament.

The Pattern of the Lord Jesus

Although it was the Lord Jesus Himself who was carrying out the ministry in the New Testament, every time He moved He did not act individually, but He brought with Him a group of people. This group of people, like the Levites who served the priests, followed the Lord, served the Lord, and took care of whatever He needed. They were those who served the Lord Jesus and His ministry.

The Practice of Paul

In Acts, particularly in Paul's ministry, in addition to those who worked together with Paul and were apostles together with him, there was still another group of people serving Paul and his work. For example, Luke (Col. 4:14), who was a doctor, followed Paul and served him as his personal physician. Besides Luke, there were others such as

Mark (2 Tim. 4:11) who also followed Paul, serving him and his ministry. Hence, the Apostle Paul also had a group of "Levites" serving him.

This is the outline of the administration of God's move in the New Testament. This is the topmost way of administration in human society. This is neither autocracy nor democracy. There is only teaching and correction; at most, administration and oversight, without lording it over or controlling. None of the political terminology ever used in human history could possibly express such a way.

The Constitution, the Basic Principle, of the Administration of God's New Testament Economy

The administration of God's New Testament economy is the topmost administration in human society. What is the constitution of God's administration? Without question, the constitution of God's administration is the sixty-six books of the Bible. This constitution was not instituted by the representatives of the people; this constitution is simply God Himself. Therefore, God's administration in the New Testament is not by human autocracy or by human democracy, but by God Himself administrating. If the apostles, elders, deacons, and all the saints are walking according to the Bible, then they are in God's administration. Otherwise, whether they are apostles or local elders or deacons or the saints, they fall outside of God's administration and bring in a situation of confusion in which they act at will. This is the situation of today's Protestantism and Catholicism; this is also the main reason we left that system. We do not wish to serve in such a situation of confusion, but rather we would forsake everything to come back to the Word of God and serve according to His Word and His desire. This is the basic principle of God's administration in His New Testament economy.

The Administration in the Lord's Recovery

In 1922 the Lord raised up His recovery in China. The one who took the lead among the first group of brothers

and was used by the Lord to release His truths was Brother
Watchman Nee. He made a thorough study of the Bible
and possessed spiritual insight and knowledge of God. He
collected many writings in Christianity concerning church
history, the establishing of different denominations, biog-
raphies of famous men, and the writings by the great
teachers. There were about three thousand volumes.
Therefore, he was not merely enlightened by the Bible to
see God's New Testament economy and the administration
in this economy; he also compared the ways of administration in the different denominations and Christian
groups in the last two thousand years. He had seen the
proper practice of God's New Testament economy, and he
practiced the church life according to what he had seen, as
I have mentioned briefly before. At the same time, there
was a group of brothers and sisters like Levites helping
him in order to put into print what he had seen. Whenever
he opened his mouth to give a message, there were some who
would do the recording, transcribing, and polishing. The
messages were reviewed by him, then typeset, printed, and
published. This was our past practice in mainland China.

In 1949 we were led by the Lord to move from the
mainland to Taiwan. According to the Lord's leading in
the past among us, that is, according to God's administration which we have followed, we began to have local
churches, the work of the apostles, and those who serve the
apostles and their work. At present, the Lord's recovery
has spread to six continents and has more than nine
hundred churches, requiring the service of more Levites.
My ministry alone occupies about sixty full-timers, who
serve in the three ministry stations in Anaheim, California,
and Irving, Texas, in the United States, and Taipei, Taiwan.
Besides these, there are many who volunteer to serve. In
the full-timers' training this time there are many from
abroad who volunteered to come to help in meal preparation,
construction, cleaning, and translation. Therefore, now in
Taipei we can see the model of the administration in God's
New Testament economy. Here we have the church, the
work of the apostles, and the service of the Levites.

THE MANAGEMENT OF FINANCES
IN GOD'S ADMINISTRATION

Because of the fact that it requires money to carry out anything on this earth, there is the matter of finances. There is no definite rule or guide regarding this matter in the Bible. There is no such thing as controlling finances, nor setting up a department to manage finances. According to the principle in the Bible, the management of finances is carried out spontaneously, not requiring the setting up of a center for management. If this is done, there will be much harm. At the present, there are nearly one thousand serving the Lord full time in Taiwan. According to the way of Christianity, there would definitely be the need to set up a mission to handle all the monetary offerings. Everything would need to pass through that mission and be distributed by it. But we cannot do things that way. The proper situation among us should be that no matter which church produces the full-timers, whether these full-timers stay in that same city or go to work in other localities, the church which produces the full-timers should be before the Lord to follow His leading concerning the matter of supporting them. In this way man's flesh will not have any opportunity to exercise control, and those who receive the support will not have the sense that they are being hired, that they cannot move freely. For example, many full-time brothers and sisters are now working in Taipei; yet they are being supported by other churches. The church in Taipei only receives the benefit of their work without bearing any financial burden for them. Without the Lord's grace, this kind of practice can never be carried out. A church may have produced a good number of full-timers, but most of them work in other localities; yet the church that produced them still supports them in love month after month. Suppose that particular church says that since those full-timers supported by them do not work in their locality, they will not support them any longer. The full-time brothers and sisters should not question, saying, "Why will you not support me when I work in another place? That will cut off my supply and I will not be able to survive." We should not have problems such as these. If you feel that you cannot survive, then you should not serve full time. If you want to serve full time, you need to do it absolutely, whether you live or die. This is the Lord's way.

I have been serving the Lord for nearly sixty years, and I have been living without definite support. If today there is something to eat, I will eat. As for tomorrow, let the Lord be responsible. In 1949, when we came from the mainland to start the work in Taiwan, we were sent by the work. However, among us, whenever the work sent someone, the work did not supply him financially. I brought all ten members of my family to Taiwan with only three hundred U.S. dollars with me, an amount sufficient for three months' living. After I had worked in Taiwan for more than ten years, I went to the United States. At that time I did not have even three hundred dollars. The brothers in the United States thought that Brother Lee was well-known everywhere and loved by many, and that those in the Far East surely had monetary offerings for him. And the brothers in the Far East thought that since Brother Lee had gone to work in a wealthy country, he surely had received much money. Eventually, neither side took much care of me. Who then took care of my living? I thank the Lord that He was the One who took care of my living. Today in the United States, the property for the two ministry stations in Anaheim and Irving alone is worth a considerable amount. Where did this come from? This was from the Lord's hand. The land was provided, and the buildings were also constructed. This is the management of finances in God's administration.

THE BELIEFS IN THE LORD'S RECOVERY

We have already seen the basic principles of administration and finances in God's New Testament economy. Following this, we need to know the beliefs in the Lord's recovery. Our beliefs are pure, orthodox, and scriptural.

First, we believe that every word in the sixty-six books of the Bible is the divine speaking revealed by God. That is, we believe that the Bible is the divine authority.

Second, we believe that the Triune God—the Father, the Son, and the Holy Spirit—is uniquely one, though three. Now He has become the Spirit and can enter into us to live in us and to be our life. Not only did He become our Savior on the cross, but today, even the more, He is the indwelling Spirit to be our life and to be with us.

Third, we believe that Jesus Christ is the Son of God, God Himself. He became a man, a God-man. This is the person of Christ. He died for us on the cross, bearing our sins and terminating all the old creation. Moreover, He rose from among the dead, releasing the life of God and producing God's new creation to be the Body of Christ. This is the work of Christ.

Fourth, we believe that the Body of Christ—the church—is unique in the entire universe, just as the moon in the sky is unique. This unique church expressed in the localities throughout the world is the many local churches. We as the members in these churches should love one another and keep the oneness of the Body of Christ.

Fifth, we believe that the Lord Jesus will come again. These are our major beliefs.

THE PRACTICE IN THE LORD'S RECOVERY

Concerning the way of practice, the work, and the meetings in the Lord's recovery, we believe that the most effective way to preach the gospel, according to the revelation in the Bible, is to take the gospel directly into people's homes by door-to-door visitation so that they may believe and be baptized to belong to the Lord. Then we establish home meetings in the homes of the saved ones to teach them the truth and lead them to grow. Gradually, when a few homes come together, they can form a small group meeting. Then a few small group meetings can form a district meeting. Next a few district meetings can gather in a larger place to meet together. These meetings in a larger meeting place with everyone coming together may be only once every few months, or twice a year. This is our way of practice at the present time. We would like to come back to the Bible and, according to what we have fellowshipped here today, practice taking care of the spreading of the gospel and have saints meeting in homes everywhere with everyone functioning. This is the way we need to take today.

A message given by Brother Witness Lee in Taipei on April 6, 1987.

CHAPTER TWO

THE MINISTRY OF GOD'S
NEW TESTAMENT ECONOMY

Scripture Reading: Acts 1:17; Eph. 4:11-12; Matt. 16:18; Phil. 2:12

I hope that all the brothers and sisters serving in the ministry station realize what it is you are serving and what is the purpose of your service.

THE NEW TESTAMENT MINISTRY

First, we need to know that our commission is the Lord's recovery on the earth. We also need to know that the Lord's recovery is absolutely different from Christianity. We are not setting up another operation or starting another work among so many works of Christianity. From the beginning we answered the Lord's call to come out from the degraded Christianity that the Bible calls the great Babylon, the great harlot. Until today, we are still outside of Christianity. The testimony that we are bearing is the testimony revealed by the Lord in the Bible.

Second, from the beginning the Lord's recovery was brought in by His ministry. This ministry is not the work of any particular brother, but is the New Testament ministry.

The New Testament ministry is not merely the work of Paul nor merely the work of Peter. The New Testament ministry was borne by the twelve apostles initially, then carried on by other apostles, among whom the most prominent one was Paul. After Paul there were still others. As apostles and co-workers, each of these brothers had his portion of work; yet they did not have many ministries.

ONE MINISTRY AND MANY MINISTERS

As far as we are concerned, the first time the New

Testament mentions this ministry is in Acts 1:17. There it says that what the twelve apostles had was this unique ministry. Paul said in 2 Corinthians that they had received this ministry (2 Cor. 4:1). Paul and his co-workers, although there were many of them, had all received the one ministry.

The beginning of the Lord's recovery was also this one ministry. In this ministry the most prominent one used by the Lord was Brother Watchman Nee. Besides him, there were other co-workers who were bearing the burden of the work of this ministry with him. Ephesians 4 says that Christ gave some apostles, and some prophets, and some evangelists, and some shepherds and teachers, for the perfecting of the saints unto the work of ministry (4:11-12). This shows us that this ministry includes even every perfected saint. As long as a person has a part in God's New Testament economy and also bears the burden of this economy with all the saints, he is in this ministry.

THE MINISTRY FOR THE BUILDING UP
OF THE BODY OF CHRIST

The four kinds of gifted persons mentioned in Ephesians chapter four are for the building up of the church to be the Body of Christ. When we speak of the church, our understanding is for the most part concerning the local aspect; however, when we speak of the Body of Christ, the emphasis is on the universal aspect. There is only one Body of Christ in the universe. The Lord's recovery is for recovering the testimony of the Body of Christ. Whoever has a part in the testimony of the Body of Christ is one who functions in the Body of Christ. It may be that many of these are not apostles, but they nevertheless have a part in the ministry borne by the apostles. They are being perfected in the Body of Christ, with each one functioning. According to Ephesians chapter four, those who build up the Body of Christ directly are not the apostles, but all the saints, that is, those members who are perfected and who are carrying out their functions. Therefore, the ministry of building up the Body of Christ can be divided into three levels: the first level is the building by Christ, the second, the building by the apostles, and the third, the direct building by the perfected saints.

THE MINISTRY BEING THE WORK
OF THE LORD'S MOVE ON THE EARTH

What is the ministry? Most people lack the proper understanding of the ministry. I often heard you pray in the meeting, saying, "We need to follow the ministry," or "We need to be one with the ministry." I doubt that you have a true understanding concerning the ministry. In the Bible, there are these two words—ministry and minister. These two are not the same. "Ministry" refers to the work of the Lord's move on the earth, whereas "minister" refers to one who bears responsibility in the Lord's work. We have spoken concerning this point quite thoroughly among us for many years.

THE MINISTRY IN THE OLD TESTAMENT

Throughout the generations there has been the work of the Lord's move. In the Old Testament, during Noah's age, the Lord's move was the building of the ark. This work of building the ark was the ministry in Noah's age. Noah was the chief minister in that ministry. However, just by Noah alone, there was no way to build the ark. At that time, there must have been some who built the ark together with Noah. The work of building the ark was the ministry in that age. Do you think that in that ministry there were two or more different works, or two or more groups of different people, or two or more different leaderships? Certainly not; otherwise, the ark could never have been built.

The problems of Christianity in the past two thousand years have been due to too many "ministries." Every denomination and every sect say that they are building the church of Christ. Many chapels have a piece of foundation stone inscribed with the words, "Christ Jesus, our foundation." One Jesus Christ is divided up into many foundations. This is the crucial point of all the problems.

The Bible shows us very clearly that in Noah's age

there was only one ministry; yet many ministers were there together building the ark. This does not mean that every minister was a master builder. Only Noah was the leader in the ministry of building the ark.

During the age of Moses, God desired to build the tabernacle with its furniture, the most important of which was the ark. Moses himself alone could not have built all those things, but he had the ministry of building the tabernacle, which was the work to fulfill God's unique purpose. In this ministry, there was not only Moses himself; Moses was one of many ministers, and, undeniably, he was the leading one in that ministry. If there had been other leaders besides Moses, there would have been confusion in that situation.

During the age of David and Solomon, God desired to build the temple. The building of the temple was not merely a work, but a ministry. At that time, there were not two different ministries building the temple; hence, there were not two different leaderships. In David's age, it was David who was taking the lead. After David passed away, Solomon was the one taking the lead. However, anyone who had a part in the ministry of building the temple, including the stone-cutters and stone-movers, was a minister in that ministry.

THE MINISTRY IN THE NEW TESTAMENT

In the New Testament, the Lord Jesus came and He said, "On this rock I will build My church" (Matt. 16:18). The first one who participated in the ministry of building the church was the Lord Jesus. The Lord's ministry was to build up the Body of Christ. For this, He chose twelve apostles and brought them into the ministry of building the church. Afterward, He also brought in other apostles, among whom the most prominent was Paul.

Since in every age there has been the work of ministry, it stands to reason that in this age also there should be the continuation of the Lord's ministry. We cannot deny that on the earth today there is the Lord's building. The Lord has been building throughout the generations, and He will continue to build until His building work is fully completed, when the New Jerusalem descends from heaven.

A CHRISTIAN NEEDING TO BE
IN THE LORD'S MINISTRY IN THIS AGE

Now we have already seen clearly that the ministry spoken of in the Bible does not refer to a person, but to God's building work. Moreover, in God's building ministry, there are those who take the lead in that ministry in every age. May the Lord open our eyes to see that as long as we are human beings, we should be Christians; as long as we are Christians, we should enter into the Lord's ministry in this age.

Today there are thousands of people who believe in the Lord Jesus and are saved, but not many have entered into the Lord's ministry of building the church. It is just like the situation in Noah's age. There were thousands of people on the earth, but only a small number were building the ark with Noah. This is why Philippians 2:12 says, "Work out your own salvation with fear and trembling." What Noah and those who built the ark with him were doing was to work out their own salvation. Yes, it was God who had saved them, but the ark that delivered them was built with their own hands by God's grace. Today, we also need to be in God's building ministry to work out our own salvation, that is, to bring our salvation to its ultimate conclusion so that we can be exalted by God in glory as the Lord Jesus was.

A PERSONAL TESTIMONY

When I was saved over sixty years ago, there were Christians all around me; yet I had no knowledge of God's move on the earth. I thank God that He gave me a heart that loves the Bible. I read it continually and even collected many reference books. Afterward, I became very clear that as a human being, I must be a Christian, and as a Christian, I must be in God's move. Therefore, I dropped everything and dove into the Lord's recovery. At that time, although I could not speak the message that I am giving this morning, the vision within me was very clear. I saw that there was the Lord's commission upon Brother Nee, which is the ministry. I also knew that Brother Nee was the one chosen, commissioned by the Lord in this age to bring in His recovery. I therefore recognized him as the leader in this work.

THE PROBLEMS IN THE LORD'S RECOVERY BEING DUE TO THE MATTER OF LEADERSHIP

After I came into the Lord's recovery, having dropped my job, Brother Nee wanted me to join his work, and he committed to me a considerable amount of responsibility. At that time, there were quite a few brothers who had been in the Lord's recovery longer than I, and they were also older in age. I was a young person who had just come in. I did not know why Brother Nee entrusted me with that much. Afterward, I began to understand that those brothers all wanted to do a work which was also for the Lord's recovery, but whenever Brother Nee had a certain leading, there were some who had other opinions so that it was difficult for Brother Nee to carry out the work in the Lord's recovery. Therefore, the speed of progress of the Lord's recovery during that period was not quite what we expected. In China, from the south to the north, there were many who responded to Brother Nee's books. Ten thousand copies of each issue of the magazine, "The Christian," were published. But very few would truly take the way that Brother Nee saw and would work together with him under his leadership. Not many had really seen the leadership in the Lord's recovery.

For this reason, right from the start of the Lord's recovery in China, there was the problem with the matter of leadership. In 1922, when the Lord's recovery just began, the two other co-workers who served with Brother Nee were fighting for leadership. And in 1924, they even signed a paper together to cut off Brother Nee. In 1927, the Lord opened the door for Brother Nee in Shanghai, and the meetings began there. A new group of brothers came in. They were not like the first group of people who fought for leadership. Outwardly, this second group all accepted Brother Nee's leadership, but nearly all of them had their own opinions when they did things together.

In 1942, the work of Brother Nee encountered a storm. The storm was so great that Brother Nee could not minister for six years. In 1946, I brought the revival in northern China to Shanghai, and Shanghai also had a revival. This revival paved a way for Brother Nee to recover his ministry by the spring of 1948. Over ninety percent of those who opposed Brother Nee confessed and repented, and they were willing to accept Brother Nee's leadership from then on. Brother Nee said, "If you want me to take the lead from now on, everyone has to hand himself over." To hand over oneself means to have no opinions. This is to say that Brother Nee led only those who were without opinions. Therefore, everyone formally wrote a slip of paper to hand himself over to Brother Nee, to accept his leadership.

THE MOVE OF THE LORD'S RECOVERY OVERSEAS

In 1949 I came to Taiwan due to the unstable situation in mainland China. Before I came to Taiwan, southeast Asia was the only place overseas that had local churches, and the total number was less than one hundred. Now there are nearly nine hundred churches in the six continents of the earth. When the Lord's recovery came to the United States, the things that attracted the American brothers the most were the truths and the life supply in the Lord's recovery. These two items attracted them to come into the Lord's recovery. Among those who came in during that time were college students and preachers. Nevertheless, there were a small number who held different opinions and eventually left us.

In 1972 and 1973 the Lord's recovery in the United States began to spread through migration; the number of saints increased greatly. Many came in, and much opinion came in as well. In those years, some problems also arose in the United States. All the problems were due to opinions. Therefore, in 1982 I called an international elders' meeting to do my best to help the brothers. In 1984 and 1985 I continued to call for international elders' meetings. I said, "For the Lord's recovery to spread on the earth, there cannot be any opinions, and everyone must be in one accord. The most important thing today is the oneness. Everyone needs to be in one accord, to blow one trumpet and accept one leadership." I hope that by my speaking these words, you can see that the hindrances and losses we encountered in the Lord's recovery in the last sixty years have all been due to different opinions. These opinions and arguments had almost nothing to do with the truth, but were related to the practices.

In one of the meetings in February of 1986, I formally announced, "I have tolerated the situation of discord in the United States for over twenty years already. From now on, I will not tolerate any longer." This does not mean that if you are not in one accord, then you are not a local church. You are still a local church, but you will have difficulty working together with me. I am like Gideon blowing the trumpet. It does not mean that those who did not follow Gideon were not Israelites, but it means that those who did not follow Gideon could not be ranked within the army of Gideon. I have received a burden from the Lord, and this burden requires the co-workers to move in one accord.

THE SERVICE OF THE MINISTRY STATION HELPING WITH THE SPREAD OF THE MINISTRY

Now I want to talk about the ministry station. Although here in Taiwan the name "The Gospel Book Room" is used, what we have here is still a part of the ministry station. The ministry station is composed of the Levites who serve the ministry. We all should see that the fact that the churches on the earth today can be established and supplied is altogether due to this ministry. And this ministry can become widespread, for the most part, due to the help rendered through the Levitical service in the ministry station. Suppose for these twenty years I had gone to the United States, and there had been no issue of publications, cassette tapes, or video tapes. In that case, the spread of the ministry would have been reduced by more than one-half. The expansion of this ministry depends not only on the effectiveness of the ministry itself, but also on the effectiveness manifested by the coordination between the work of the Levites in the ministry station and the ministry. This also indicates the importance of the ministry station.

THE BASIC PRINCIPLES
OF SERVING IN THE MINISTRY STATION
Without Opinion

There are a few basic principles of serving in the ministry station: first, no opinions are allowed, and second, everyone accepts one leadership. Although the ministry station is separated into three offices—Anaheim, Irving, and Taipei—there is only one management, one leadership. The ministry station has its direction and method of management. Those who come to serve all know clearly that they should only serve and not have any opinion. It does not matter how foolish or how poor the decisions of the ministry station seem to you, as long as you are one who comes in to serve, you must do things according to that way, and you cannot bring in your opinions. According to my experience, no matter how good the way is, once there are opinions, the matters will be ruined. The way may be somewhat foolish; yet it will be all right if there are no opinions.

In the beginning when I was leading the church in Taipei, I purposely worked to reach a point that no one had any opinion. When the elders came together, every one was positive, without any opinions. They were all of one heart. Hence, the Lord's work in the first few years was becoming more prosperous day after day, and the number of believers increased continually. Therefore, I set up a basic principle for the ministry station that whoever comes to serve cannot bring any opinions. Of course, we are not capable in every aspect, but we have our own way. If you follow our way, you will succeed at the end.

Be in One Accord and Love One Another

I also desire that the service in the ministry station be harmonious. There needs to be harmony in order to have a testimony. Like those who helped Moses build the tabernacle, our Levites who help the ministry should have a testimony of oneness. Those who serve in the ministry station are not allowed to have discord. This ministry is for the building of the church. Naturally, the Levites who serve the ministry need to have the testimony of the ministry. I hope that those who serve in the ministry station can be in one accord and also love one another.

Now the Lord's recovery is spreading abroad; the service of the Levites is increasing on all sides. From now on, we should not make distinctions between people; we all are the serving ones of the one ministry. Here there are no seniors or juniors; there is neither high rank nor low rank. We have only one management, one administration. In this service we have no opinions, and we do not care for right or wrong; we simply love one another and are harmonious together. We really feel that our commission is too great. May the fellowship today be of benefit to us and give grace within.

A message given by Brother Witness Lee in Taipei on May 14, 1987.

CHAPTER THREE

THE SERVING ONES OF THE MINISTRY OF GOD'S NEW TESTAMENT ECONOMY

Scripture Reading: Eph. 4:11-12; Col. 1:25-27

We have already seen that the administration of the Lord's move on the earth began with the apostles and the apostles' ministry. Out of that ministry the church is produced. On the side of the church, there is the service of the church; on the side of the ministry, there is the work of the ministry. In the work of the ministry there is the service of the Levites, as typified in the Old Testament. Without the help of the Levites and their service, it would have been difficult to carry out the priestly ministry in the Old Testament. Although, on the spiritual side, what the Levites did was not as weighty as what the priests did, yet on the practical side, both what the Levites did and what the priests did were necessary. You may compare the priesthood of the priests to the inward life, and the work of the Levites to the outward body. Without the body, it would be difficult for life to exist; without life, the body would be merely an empty shell. The life and the body need to match each other.

In the Lord's recovery, we have seen the sketch and framework of this matter very clearly from the first day. The light which the Lord has given us is becoming brighter and brighter. After passing through more than sixty years, today you may say that it is completely clear. Not only have we seen the light from the Bible, but we have also checked with the history of Christianity and our own sixty years of experience, especially the Lord's leading given to us in the last thirty years, along with the many admonitions and warnings we have received through our practice. Therefore, we have a very thorough understanding concerning this matter.

THE SPREAD OF THE LORD'S RECOVERY
RELYING HEAVILY ON PUBLICATIONS
AND ON AUDIO AND VIDEO TAPES

After World War II, due to the worldwide economic prosperity, the ease of transportation, and the improvement in communication media, we have been enjoying a greater convenience than before in transmitting information. Formerly, it took half a day to make an overseas phone call, but now through the international long distance telephone, in a short time we can have a thorough discussion of affairs among a number of overseas churches. In the past, when Brother Nee released messages, there were no microphones, nor any tape recordings. The messages were recorded in shorthand, which often was not perfect. Today, we have both audio-tape and video-tape recordings; all the messages can be conveniently preserved. In 1958, I began to visit the western world. Although for the most part I have worked in the United States, through the publications, audio tapes, and video tapes, the messages in the Lord's recovery have been spread to the six continents of the earth. Many seeking ones in different countries have received supplies of these publications, audio tapes, and video tapes.

We compiled some statistics three years ago that showed there were altogether over six hundred churches in the Lord's recovery throughout the whole earth. Recently, we estimated that the number of churches has increased to over nine hundred. Within this three-year period, most of the three hundred newly added churches were outside of the Far East. The raising up of the church in each place was mainly through the issuing of publications and the distribution of audio and video tapes, not through the co-workers' going out to work. The video tapes, at present, are the most practical. In Mexico, we have eight or nine video stations. Through the release of the messages station by station, about twenty churches have been raised up. Although the Spanish-speaking saints also emphasize publications, unfortunately the Spanish translation work is still falling behind due to the limitation of time and manpower.

Recently I received a letter from Paraguay in South America requesting two hundred fifty sets of Life-studies at one time. Another letter came from a brother who was a preacher in the Republic of Ecuador in South America. This brother's work was quite effective. He had already baptized over two thousand people and had established over twenty churches. He said that his sister had led him to see this way, and now he needed the truth materials to supply those under his leading. He presented this need to us and asked us to supply him. Even people from India have also requested our publications. It has been due to the supply of these publications and video tapes that the Lord's recovery has been able to spread rapidly to the six continents.

Today, on the spiritual side, there is drought, desolation, and famine over the whole earth. This is the main reason that all the saints in every place over the whole globe are so thirsty for the publications and video tapes in the Lord's recovery. In 1962 I spoke publicly in the United States, saying, "Since the end of World War II, whether in Europe or America, not many spiritual books have been published that have spiritual light and spiritual weight such that people can receive the supply in life and edification in the truth." In the last century, especially in England, spiritual books were mushrooming like bamboo shoots after rain, being published in bundles. However, after World War II, it has no longer been the same.

Among us today there are a good number of brothers from the United States; they all have to admit that even in such a vast Christian country as the United States, people are suffering spiritual famine. The Lord's recovery has been able to spread overseas mainly because of the truth. Besides the churches in the Far East, the raising up of over five hundred other churches has been for the most part due to the issuing of publications, audio tapes, and video tapes in the Lord's recovery.

THE ESTABLISHING OF THE MINISTRY STATION FOR THE PROPAGATION OF THE TRUTH

For this reason, the ministry station needs many more

people to come to serve. At the beginning of April this year, I was writing the *Life Lessons* in Taipei. Originally I only hoped that the Chinese edition could be quickly translated into English after it was issued; that would have been good enough. Never would I have thought that among the trainees who came to Taipei from different countries, we could find some translators who could together translate the "Mystery of Human Life" from Chinese into thirty-four different languages. At present, some of them are still continuing the translation work and beginning to translate the forty-eight lessons of the *Life Lessons* into twenty-seven languages. Of these, about eighteen languages have already been completed, in order to meet the needs of different countries. A few years ago, in the ministry station we considered gathering all the editors into one place so that as soon as the messages come out, they could immediately be translated into different languages so that the truths could be quickly spread abroad. Our purpose in establishing the ministry station was for the propagation of the truths. In this respect, we have already seen a great effect at the present time.

Today, the Lord's speaking is clearly in His recovery. The saved ones in every place and many who are hungry for the Lord desire the truth and the understanding of the Bible. Therefore, when our publications went into places such as North and South Africa, and Central and South America, those who pursue the truth were eager to receive them. The greatest need now is for the ministry station to quickly put out the publications, audio tapes, and video tapes. The audio and video tapes are being used extensively, and the results they produce are also very significant.

At present we are promoting the new way of going out to preach the gospel by door-to-door visitation and establishing home meetings. This has created a very great need. When we go to preach the gospel by knocking on doors and go to lead home meetings, it is not adequate only to speak with our mouths; it is best to give each one a book and lead him to read it. It is even better to give him an audio tape so that he can listen to it again and again. If there are publications available for reading and audio tapes for listening, it will be easy for people to get into the truths. Our ministry station needs to do its best to supply people with publications and audio tapes.

In the New Testament, Paul also had a group of people serving him, although he did not use the term "ministry station." It was the same with the Lord Jesus when He was on the earth; even His food supply was taken care of by that group of serving ones. Now the Lord's recovery has spread to the six major continents; there are those everywhere who love the Lord and hunger after the Lord's truth. This urgent need is something that we have no way to take care of fully. It does not mean that we have no supply; rather, we have the top supply here, but these supplies are not fully distributed yet.

THE COOPERATION OF THE CHURCH
WITH THE MINISTRY

The raising up of the work of the ministry and of the ministry station is entirely for the establishing of churches. If the churches cooperate with the ministry and the ministry station, their effectiveness will definitely increase significantly. Due to the extensive need, the ministry must have a group of serving ones. Today, the ministry station is set up in three places: Anaheim, Irving, and Taipei, with over sixty brothers and sisters altogether. They are a group of serving ones serving the ministry, cooperating with the ministry to distribute the truths and the publications. We expect to find many more capable ones in order to meet this urgent need.

Besides these needs, there is now in addition the full-time training being held here in Taipei. More than five hundred attended this training last semester, and over one thousand this semester. Over three hundred came from abroad, from approximately twenty-three countries. In order to meet the need for dormitories, we even purchased eleven units in the building next to Hall Three and spent a total of fifty million Taiwan dollars. This amount was offered mainly by the overseas Chinese-speaking brothers.

We really saw the Lord's confirmation in that, although the expenses were great, the Lord's supply was abundant. In order to cooperate with this training, the main personnel of the two ministry stations in the United States were transferred to Taipei for remodeling Hall Three and Hall One to meet the urgent need. Although we tried our best to avoid entangling the church, we had no other way, because we needed to use the church property as a training facility and the church members as coordinating personnel. I thank the Lord that the local churches are indeed cooperative. Not only did they send people to coordinate and serve, but they also allowed the training to have the full use of the facilities.

The training here in Taipei has been set up by the ministry for the perfecting of the churches. We need the whole church to rise up to coordinate for the goal of gospelizing Taiwan in five years. Everything the work of the ministry accomplishes is for the benefit of the churches. Whatever is carried out here by this training belongs one hundred percent to the churches in Taiwan. There is no difference whether you come from the churches or the ministry station; we all need to put our shoulders to the work. We are in one accord doing whatever needs to be done in every aspect spontaneously and automatically.

I would let you all know that the reason we have such an effect today is not due to the labor of one person, but is the result of continual development through the past sixty years. The greater part of my work is a continuation of that of Brother Watchman Nee. It was the Gospel Book Room that served him in his ministry. Besides that, no one else served him and his ministry.

In 1950, Brother Nee arrived in Hong Kong and wanted me to come from Taiwan to see him. When he fellowshipped about the matter of issuing publications, he took the opportunity to make some arrangements. It was decided that the Gospel Book Room would remain one, yet due to the political situations, it had to conduct business separately in three places: Shanghai, Taipei, and Hong Kong. Brother Nee was responsible for the bookroom in

Shanghai, I was responsible for the one in Taipei, and Brother Weigh was responsible for the one in Hong Kong. However, Brother Nee wanted me also to take care of the responsibility for the publications of the Hong Kong book- room. In addition, he made it clear that the finances of the bookroom in each place should be taken care of by each respective place. Also, he provided a very clear leading from the beginning that all the finances related to the ministry should be clearly separated from those of the church; they should not be mixed together. The ministry does not interfere with the finances of the church, and the church does not interfere with the finances of the bookroom. What is of the bookroom is altogether related to the ministry, and not to the church. Therefore, when we first started the work here on Jen Ai Road, we made very clear and appropriate arrangements regarding the usage of the meeting hall by both the bookroom and the church, as well as the division of the property rights.

THE MINISTRY STATION NOT HAVING
ANY WORLDLY ORGANIZATION

Through sixty years of practice, we have learned the lesson not to rely on organization. Therefore, strictly speaking, we do not have organization, and we have no desire to have anyone to be the head. In the past, when Brother Nee was taking the lead, he never took the position of the head, as in a worldly organization. Today, among the three ministry stations, although I have the ground to do all the speaking, I have no desire to speak on the ground of organization. I hope that such a situation will not exist among us. All those who come to serve in the ministry station need to have a heart of consecration. Furthermore, only those who are recognized by our bookroom as suitable can be accepted to serve. In the United States, especially in Irving, many brothers and sisters who come to serve in the ministry station are not the so-called employees, but volunteers who do not receive any compensation or support. Of course, we know the needs of some and will take care of them. Therefore, the service of the ministry station is not like a worldly organization hiring some employees to do the work. Rather, it is all the serving ones consecrating themselves, for the sake of loving the Lord, and each exercising his ability to do what he can do and what he should do.

THE FORMING OF THE MINISTRY STATION

From 1949 when I came from mainland China to start the work in Taiwan, until 1961 when I turned to the United States, we had only the Gospel Book Room in Taiwan publishing my writings. There was no service of the ministry station yet. After I started the work in the United States in 1962, the Stream Publishers was established in 1963 in Los Angeles to publish the messages I released in the United States. Brother Samuel Chang, who has since gone to the Lord, took charge of this for eleven years. In 1974 we moved from Los Angeles to Anaheim, and we began to have trainings twice a year, summer and winter, specifically for the Life-study of the Bible. This caused the business affairs among us to increase, and the ministry station was formed in order to meet the need. From that time on, we began to publish the Life-study Messages, one each week. In 1976, the church in Anaheim and the ministry station finished the construction of the meeting hall in Anaheim; then the ministry station began to conduct business from there. The business activities gradually spread and increased. Also the serving ones in the ministry station had their views broadened and saw the future of the ministry station and the need of the Lord's recovery. They developed the issuing of audio and video tapes and kept expanding until they reached the situation of today, where there are three stations in Anaheim, Irving, and Taipei to carry on the business activities. The main business activity of the Anaheim station is the administration and the publishing, that of the Irving station is the printing of the English and Spanish publications, and that of the Taipei station is the publishing of the Chinese literature. Although there are three stations, there is only one management, presided over by one administration.

In the United States, the Irving station in Texas has its business office located in the large building jointly built by the church in Irving and the ministry station. Starting from 1982, the annual winter training for the Life-studies has been held there. Hence, beginning from 1983, Anaheim has had only the annual summer training.

THE COORDINATION OF
THE THREE MINISTRY STATIONS

Although the three ministry stations are located far apart from one another, because of the convenience of telecommunication, along with the harmonious coordination between the personnel working in Anaheim and in Irving, all the serving ones would give themselves to serve together wherever the need is. Hence, there is no sense of distinction between them. I hope that those who are serving here in Taipei will also have no feeling of strangeness toward those who came from the other two stations and will completely eliminate any concept of distinctions. We three stations are one group of people with everything the same, without any distinctions. For example, Hall One is having a major remodeling, and the serving ones from the two stations of Anaheim and Irving have come. If you see any place that needs to be swept or cleaned as you are going in and out here, you should do it spontaneously. Not only should the serving ones of the ministry station do this, but those in the local churches are needed also, if they can come to coordinate to help together. Even if you can come only to move a few pieces of brick or to empty the trash, it is a very beautiful thing.

I hope that you all are clear, first, that we have no organization. Second, we all come here to serve because of our love toward the Lord. Third, you should not think that only if you have a certain position do you have a certain responsibility, and if you do not have any position, you do not have any responsibility. Fourth, concerning those who are from overseas, regardless of whether they are from the churches in different localities or from the ministry station, all of us are one group of people and should not have any distinctions. We are very clear with respect to the truth that the church is the church, and the ministry is the ministry. The ministry is for the perfecting of the church, and the church cooperates with the ministry. In financial matters there should be a clear separation between the church and the ministry. However, concerning the cooperation needed for the accomplishment of the Lord's work, the two should work together.

GRASPING THE OPPORTUNITY TO LIVE OUT THE BODY OF CHRIST

Today the Lord has given us the best opportunity here in Taipei to live out the vision we have seen concerning the Body of Christ. People have come here to attend the training from all the major continents of the whole earth. We should grasp this opportunity to have contact and fellowship with the brothers and sisters from overseas to understand the blessed situation of every place. It is as if we are living in a big family. As far as finances are concerned, our affairs are very clearly separated room by room. But when outsiders come to knock on the door, no matter who they are looking for, it is this family's matter. Whoever hears the knock will come out to answer the door. What people see concerning us should be one family in every aspect.

I hope that the brothers in Taipei, whether elders or co-workers, or those serving in the ministry station or the bookroom, or full-time brothers and sisters, can properly express the Body of Christ. It is correct that as far as procedures for handling business and financial relationships are concerned, the ministry and the church are clearly separated. However, when we come to serve together, we are one group of people bearing God's commission together.

What we are doing today is to cause the Lord's recovery on the earth to be perfected, and to allow the Lord's recovery to spread out from us. We thank the Lord that at the end of this age, He has raised up His recovery on the earth, and has also chosen us and put us in His recovery.

Moreover, through the advancement of science and technology, with the convenience of transportation, He caused these things to work for the Lord's recovery. Although we are weak and unworthy, the Lord nevertheless has brought His recovery to every place on this earth through us. This time the Lord has brought so many brothers and sisters from every country to coordinate and serve together with us. We look to the Lord for His visitation that we may be filled with God Himself and with reality in all our services. I hope that we can all be under this burden to offer our prayer always.

A message given by Brother Witness Lee in Taipei on April 8, 1987.

Chapter Four

THE WORD OF THE LORD
AND THE SPIRIT OF THE LORD

Scripture Reading: John 1:1, 14; 6:63; 20:22

EIGHT IMPORTANT TERMS IN THE GOSPEL OF JOHN

First let us read a few verses from the Bible. John 1:1 says, "In the beginning was the Word, and the Word was with God, and the Word was God." There are two important terms in this verse: the Word and God. Verse 14 says, "The Word became flesh and tabernacled among us ... full of grace and reality." This verse adds three more important terms: flesh, grace, and reality. Chapter six, verse 63, says, "The words which I have spoken unto you are spirit and are life." This verse also adds two important terms: spirit and life. Chapter twenty, verse 22, says, "And when He had said this, He breathed into them and said to them, Receive the Holy Spirit." In this verse there are also two important terms: breath and Holy Spirit.

From these four verses in the Gospel of John, we have noted eight important terms: the Word, God, flesh, grace, reality, spirit, life, and breath. You need to memorize these eight terms.

By remembering these eight important words, you will see the light. These eight items can be divided into three groups: spirit, life, and breath are one group; the Word, God, and flesh are another group; and grace and reality are a third group.

This morning I am giving these eight terms to you who are attending the training. After the training is over, when you go out to preach the gospel, you may preach eight messages consecutively with one message on each term. You need to tell people what is the Word, what is God, and what is the flesh. It may seem that these three items—the Word, God, and flesh—are very concrete; yet they became the abstract Spirit, life, and breath. The issue is grace and reality. If a person has the first six of these items, it is guaranteed that he will have the last two items of grace and reality.

In the universe, what could be better than grace? Neither could there be anything in the universe better than reality. You should enjoy grace and reality every day. How did grace and reality come? The source of grace and reality is the Word, God, flesh, spirit, life, and breath.

When we call "O Lord Jesus! O Lord Jesus!" that is our spiritual breathing. This is the reason we practice calling on the name of the Lord. This calling is the best spiritual breathing. We can either breathe deeply or in a shallow way. When we call "O Lord Jesus!" there is fresh spiritual air coming into us. In this calling we are breathing, and we are resting as well. How sweet and how fresh it is! Moreover, the result is spirit and life.

The Gospel of John is a profound book. According to the letters, this book is very simple, but according to the philosophy it contains, it is the most profound. "In the beginning was the Word, and the Word was with God, and the Word was God.... And the Word became flesh and tabernacled among us... full of grace and reality" (John 1:1, 14). These words are very simple, so that even little children can understand. However, the philosophy they contain is very profound, beyond description. If you have received something of the Lord's grace, you may be able to understand a little. Even so, you may have no way to utter what you have received, and you may not be able to utter it thoroughly.

The Lord Jesus said, "I am the resurrection and the life," and, "I am the light of the world," and again, "I am the way" (John 11:25; 8:12; 14:6). These expressions could not be more simple, yet what He was talking about in those instances is so profound that no one is able to understand fully. Therefore, you do not need to try to understand. You only need to say unceasingly, "The Lord is life, the Lord is resurrection, and the Lord is the way." Then you will receive something within.

THE LORD BEING THE WORD AND THE SPIRIT TO US

In such a profound book as the Gospel of John, the first verse of the first chapter says, "In the beginning was the Word, and the Word was with God, and the Word was God." When you read this verse, it really sounds like scriptural writings. However, in chapter 20, after the Lord Jesus had resurrected, He came into the midst of the disciples and did one thing. Everyone would think that this wonderful Savior coming back in resurrection would definitely teach the disciples with a long discourse. No one would have thought that the Lord Jesus would not give a sermon, but would breathe into them, saying, "Receive the Holy Spirit." This portion of the record does not sound at all like scriptural writings. But the mystery of the Gospel of John is right here. This mysterious book talks about this One, who was the Word and God originally, becoming flesh, passing through human living, being put to death, buried, and resurrected. Then in resurrection He came back into the midst of His disciples and breathed into them, saying, "Receive the Holy Spirit" (John 20:22). His very breath was the Holy Spirit. Therefore, we may say that the first key word in the Gospel of John is the Word, and the last key word is the Spirit. Every believer's knowledge of the Lord should emphasize these two points: the Lord is the Word and also the Spirit to us.

THE RELATIONSHIP BETWEEN GOD AND MAN BEGINNING WITH LOVE AND CONCLUDING WITH LIFE

This mysterious book of the Gospel of John talks about the relationship between God and man. Verse 16 of chapter three says, "God so loved the world." This sentence encompasses the relationship between God and man. The relationship between God and man is love, but this is only the shallow, initial relationship. The relationship between God and man begins with love and is concluded with life. God loving you is the beginning; the result is that He wants to come into you to become your life. Concerning the relationship between God and man being love, any scholar or philosopher can understand. When it comes to the matter of God entering into man to become his life, however, the philosophers will not be able to understand even after much thought, because this matter of God becoming our life is something that does not exist within the boundary of philosophy. But this book, the Gospel of John, is to show people that this God, who has a relationship with man and who loves man, has an ultimate goal of entering into man to become his life that he may live like a man and also like God. And eventually, such men would become a group of people who take God as life, live God, and express God. Yes, we are human beings, real human beings; but we are a group of human beings who take God as our life, live God, and express God. This corresponds to the record in the beginning of the Bible. In Genesis 1:26, God said, "Let us make man in our image, after our likeness." The man God created was truly a man, yet he had God's image.

When some people rebuke others, they may say, "You see, you really look like a monkey," or, "You see, you really look like a turtle." Why would anyone look like those animals? Because that one expresses the monkey or the turtle. The Chinese call the drunkards "drinking demons," and the gamblers "gambling demons." Formerly, when I was in mainland China, I even saw "opium demons" and "morphine demons." These designations are very fitting. When those gamblers were carried away with their gambling, none of them looked like human beings; they all looked like demons. It was the same with the opium-smokers. When they lay on the the bed smoking opium, every one of them really looked like a demon. They lived out the demon, and they expressed the demon. We Christians are not like that. We are those who live God. We dare not blaspheme God by saying that we are God, but we can say that for us to live is God, just like Paul said, "For to me to live is Christ" (Phil. 1:21). The profoundness of the Gospel of John lies in the fact that God enters into man to become his life, and then God is lived out through man that man may be like Him.

In the Gospels there are records of some who were

possessed by demons and who were one with demons. In our recent revision work on the Recovery Version of the New Testament, we found pronouns used in some places that were very difficult to translate. One particular term clearly refers to the demon, yet it also refers to the one possessed by a demon. Therefore, it is very difficult to determine which pronoun to use—"it" or "he." Also, is it actually the one possessed who was speaking or the demon itself speaking? This is also very hard to explain, because the demon had become that person, and that person had become the demon. The two had become one. We Christians are not demon-possessed; rather, we are filled and saturated with God. We and God, and God and we, have fully become one. Eventually, He is us, and we are Him. This is God's ultimate purpose. How could God have this deep and mysterious relationship with us? How could God carry out His work to this extent? Because first, He is the Word, and second, He is the Spirit. The issue of this is life.

CONTACTING GOD THROUGH
THE WORD AND THE SPIRIT

Today God is still a mystery. It is difficult to understand and apprehend God. But the Bible says clearly that this God who is incomprehensible and mysterious is the Word. The Greek word for "word" means the expression of the thoughts formed in the mind. Actually, what is God? Man cannot utter what God is; yet God expresses Himself through the Word, and He uses the Word to represent Himself. God said that He is the Word. Hence the Bible says, "The Word was God." In the original Greek, this sentence was, "God was the Word." Both of these expressions are correct, because in Greek both the Word and God are subjects. God is the Word, and the Word is God; these two are one. If there is only God without the Word, then man has no way to understand; if there is the Word, then God can be described and expressed.

But how could this expressed God enter into us? The Lord Jesus said, "The words which I have spoken unto you are spirit and are life." It is indeed wonderful that the word is spirit. Once the word enters into us, it becomes spirit, and it is life. Therefore, God is the Word, the Word is the Spirit, and the Spirit is life. We contact God first through the Word, and second, through the Spirit. The result is life, and life is simply the grace and reality we have enjoyed. This is my main point. Do you want to contact God? You need to know the Word. If you know the Word, the Word will become the Spirit. Once the Word in you has become the Spirit, you have life within. This life within us is the grace and reality we have enjoyed.

NEEDING TO DEAL WITH THE WORD
AND THE SPIRIT

The most important thing for the young people who came here to be trained is to deal with the Word. Where is the word of God? It is in the Bible. In the universe there is a book called "God, having spoken" (see Heb. 1:1-2), which is the Bible. The Bible is not merely the word of God; it is even the more God's speaking, that is, God's breathing (2 Tim. 3:16). God's speaking is God's breathing. Therefore, whenever you read the Bible, you need to breathe in the word of God. "In the beginning was the Word. Amen! In the beginning was the Word!" This is to breathe in. What God breathes out is the breath, and what you breathe in is also the breath. Once this breath enters into you, it is the Spirit. Christianity is too shallow. Some Christians there actually do not deal with the Spirit. Some deal with the Spirit, but in a nonsensical way by speaking in tongues. The Bible, however, shows us that the proper way is to read and pray the word of God.

The first emphasis in reading the Bible should not be to understand it. When I was newly saved at the age of nineteen, I had a strong desire to obtain knowledge, and I loved to read the Bible very much. I was resolved to understand every verse, and even every word in the Bible. But when I came to the Gospel of John, to the verse, "In the beginning was the Word," I was stumped by this sentence. What is the beginning? I searched many reference books, but still did not understand. Furthermore, did the Chinese character for "Word" in that verse refer to the same Chinese character used for doctrine, or for morality, or for pathway? I studied, but at the end, I still did not get anything. I thought I could study the Bible the way I studied Chinese classical writings. Eventually I discovered that man can understand Chinese classical writings, but he has no way to understand the Bible.

Then what shall you do? If you do not understand, do not try to understand. Pray-read one portion—"In the beginning was the Word, and the Word was with God, and the Word was God. Amen! The Word was God. Amen! In the beginning. Amen! In the beginning was the Word. Amen! Was the Word. Hallelujah!" If you pray-read in this way, after only ten minutes, you will be satisfied within. This is the best way to read the Bible.

The Bible is God's breathing out, so that you can breathe it in. This Word is God, and it is the breath. When you breathe this breath into you, it becomes the Spirit. Once it becomes the Spirit, it is life. This life becomes the grace and reality in your daily living. This is the Lord's salvation. This is not religion. Religion's way can be compared to teaching a child not to tell lies. Soon after such a lesson, the child will commit some wrongdoing and then immediately fabricate a story to tell you another lie. Hence, such teaching is useless. Rather, we need to lead the little children to pray-read the Lord's word and let this word become the breath to enter into them. This breath entering into them is the Spirit. The Spirit becomes life, and this life within them is the grace and the reality. Then when such a child wants to do something wrong, within him something will not allow him to do it, rather, will require him to abide in reality. As a result, what he lives out will be God. This is altogether different from religion.

I hope that you would practice dealing with the word and the Spirit every day. To deal with the word is to read the Bible; to deal with the Spirit is to pray. You may say that you do not have many words to pray with. Actually, the entire Bible is your prayer book. You can turn to any page and use it to pray. When you read the Bible, you are dealing with the word; when you pray, you are dealing with the Spirit. Eventually, the word and the Spirit become life, which is your enjoyment and your gain. This enjoyment and gain are grace and reality.

A message given by Brother Witness Lee in Taipei on August 20, 1987.

CHAPTER FIVE

THE VISION OF THE BODY OF CHRIST

(1)

Scripture Reading: Eph. 1:23; 2:16; 3:6; 4:4, 11-12, 16;
Col. 1:18, 24; 3:15; Rom. 12:4-5; 1 Cor. 12:12-13, 18, 24-25;
10:17; 11:29

THE NEED TO SEE THE VISION
OF THE BODY OF CHRIST

Beginning with this message, I hope that the Lord will
grant us grace that we can see the Body of Christ. This is
something that has never been talked about in human
history or human culture outside of the Bible. We need to
see the vision of the Body of Christ. A vision is a view, but
it is not common. Rather it is extraordinary, unusual,
something that man does not ordinarily see, nor is able to
see. Every one of us who is saved, especially every one who
loves the Lord, follows the Lord, and learns to live to Him
and serve Him, needs to see such a vision.

Such a vision does not exist among the Gentiles.
Neither is there such a vision found in the Gentile books,
even in the so-called classical writings. Confucius' philosophy was very proper. Besides the Bible, it is the most
respectable philosophy among all the philosophies, without much mixture or fables or unclean things. Although
he did not say much about God, Confucius nevertheless
had some words expressing his viewpoint concerning God.
He definitely believed that there is a Supreme Being in the
universe. However, he had not received any revelation to
see Christ, nor had he received any vision to see that
Christ has a Body in the universe. Such a wise and pure
one as Confucius did not even speak concerning this
matter; even the more, there is no need to mention other
classical writings.

When the Lord Jesus was on the earth, although He mentioned the church in Matthew chapter sixteen, He did not speak concerning His Body because He knew that the time was not ripe yet. When the Apostle Paul was raised up by the Lord, he began to receive revelation to see the vision of the Body of Christ, and he released some unique messages based on this vision. Not only was he different from the prophets in the Old Testament, but he was also different from the other apostles in the New Testament. The focal point of the uniqueness of the messages he released was the one Body of Christ. There were more than forty writers of the sixty-six books of the Bible, but only this writer Paul spoke concerning the Body of Christ. This expression was created uniquely by Paul. His usage of the expression "the Body of Christ" was very deep, emphatic, and profound.

THE BODY OF CHRIST BEING A REALITY

Some Bible teachers consider the Body of Christ spoken of by Paul as an illustration or a figure of speech. But according to the important verses in the New Testament concerning the Body of Christ as cited in this message, we can see clearly that the Body of Christ is not a figure of speech, but a reality. In the universe, there is definitely a Body—not your body or my body—but the Body of Christ. This is a fact. Hence, 1 Corinthians 11:29 says, "Not discerning the body." The Bible translators in early days did not understand the meaning. Therefore the Chinese Union Version added the word "the Lord's" to make the translation read, "Not discerning the Lord's body." Actually, it should be translated as, "Not discerning the body." What Paul meant to tell us here is that there is something unique in the universe that we need to discern, that is, the Body of Christ. The Body of Christ is a unique thing; it is not a figure of speech, but a reality, an existing fact.

THE FOUR GREAT PERSONS IN THE BIBLE

I once pointed out that the Bible mentions four great persons. First, the Old Testament mentions God. God is the unique and foremost great Person in the Bible. All the thirty-nine books of the Old Testament talk about God. Second, in the New Testament the four Gospels begin to speak of Christ. Third, the book of Acts and the Epistles talk about another great person, the church. The church is the Body of Christ, and Christ is the One who fills all in all (Eph. 1:23). He is so great that even if you add together the different words used at all times and all places for describing greatness, such as grandeur and magnificence, they are still not adequate for describing Christ. The greatness of Christ is unspeakable. Therefore, in the prayer in Ephesians chapter three, Paul prayed that God would enable us to apprehend what is the breadth and length and height and depth of the universe (v. 18). The height of the universe is unlimited, and its breadth and length and depth are also unlimited. The measurements of this unlimitedness are Christ. Christ is the One who fills all in all, yet the church is His Body.

Therefore, in the universe, there is such a One whom no modifiers can describe. First, He is God, then He is Christ, and then He is the Body of Christ. The embodiment of God is Christ. Outside of Christ you cannot find God. God has embodied Himself in Christ, and Christ also became the church. The church is the embodiment of Christ. Hence, in his Epistles in the New Testament Paul says, "The mystery of God, Christ" (Col. 2:2). Paul also says that the mystery of Christ is the church (Eph. 3:4, 6). Finally, at the end of the New Testament, there is the fourth great person, the bride, which is also the New Jerusalem.

Today, we are neither in the Old Testament, nor in the Gospels. And we are not yet in Revelation. We are in the Epistles. The first stage, which occupies the entire Old Testament, is God. The second stage, which occupies the four Gospels, is Christ. The last stage, which occupies the last book, Revelation, is the bride, the New Jerusalem. Today we are in the third stage, the stage of the Body of Christ. This occupies the twenty-two books from Acts to Jude.

THE ECONOMY OF GOD BEING
TO OBTAIN THE BODY OF CHRIST

God's economy is God's administration, and God's administration is God's plan, arrangement, intention, and work. The goal of God's economy is the Body of Christ. Some would say, "God wants sinners like me. God loves me, and God wants me." This is not wrong, but this is a near-sighted view. Not only does God want you and me; God wants every one. God wants the Chinese; He also wants the Japanese. God loves all the people in the world.

In the universe God did something extremely unusual. He scattered those whom He had chosen and predestinated before the ages among different tongues, tribes, peoples, and nations. Every one of them has an unusual temperament, a peculiar character. There is no need to speak of the problems between nations or between classes, problems that make it difficult for people to live together; even between next-door neighbors or husbands and wives, there are many problems that make it difficult for them to live together. However, the wonderful thing is that God also sent the Holy Spirit to gather us one by one and put us together, so that we have no way to escape being mingled and built together.

Due to today's advancement of world civilization, the development of science and technology, and the convenience in communication, the distance between peoples has been shortened. Formerly, it was very difficult for the Chinese to go to the United States. The United States government allotted an annual quota of only one hundred five for the Chinese immigrants. Even those who were able to come to the United States were looked down upon. It was very difficult for the Americans and Chinese to mingle together. There was an impression toward the Chinese that they were like the Cantonese that came to the United States in the early days who worked as coolies and smoked opium. In addition, the official papers put out by the China Inland Mission reported only negative aspects. Therefore, for the most part the Americans despised the Chinese people and looked down on them. However, due to World

War II, the entire situation was changed. President Roosevelt proposed the rebuilding of the international order, completely eliminating all the unequal treaties among nations. He also recommended self-rule, equality, and freedom for every nation. Based on this concept, in 1967 the immigration law of the United States was changed so that there is no longer any racial discrimination, and equal treatment is given to each nation. Then, in addition, there is the convenience of transportation shortening the distance between the United States and China. The whole situation has been completely opened. In the last two or three years, the brothers and sisters among us have traveled back and forth between the United States and Taiwan frequently. People have come here to Taiwan from all six major continents of the earth that we may all be mingled together.

Formerly, there was discrimination even among those of the same country, not to say among those of different nations. When I was young, I saw that those in my home town would despise those who were merely one hundred fifty miles west of us, even though we were still in the same province. When I first arrived in Shanghai fifty years ago, as soon as those in the stores heard me speaking the northern dialect, they looked down on me. Those who lived in neighboring provinces like Shantung and Kiangsu looked down on one another; how much more was this the case with those who lived in other provinces. Since we left our country in 1948 to come to Taiwan, we had no choice but to come to meet together. When we prayed and fellowshipped together in the meeting, there were different kinds of accents. In the beginning, when brothers and sisters were considering marriage, it would make a difference where each one came from. The northerners were not entirely willing to marry the southerners. Those in one province were not willing to marry the ones from outside their province. But gradually, after more than ten years, everyone was blended together. In these years when I came back, I saw that no one cares for this matter any longer. This is God's doing. He brought us together and blended us together so that in this universe He could obtain the Body of Christ.

TO BE A UNIVERSAL CHRISTIAN

Formerly, you could be a Christian in a locality with your door closed and not be bothered with the brothers and sisters in other places. Today, however, for you to be a Christian, it is not sufficient to be a national Christian, nor even an international Christian; you need to be a universal Christian.

Three years ago when I came back to Taiwan to change the system, I had no intention of letting the American brothers know what I was doing. I told them to allow me first to go back to Taiwan, and that whatever I did there, they would gradually find out. But they followed right behind and came all the way to Taiwan. Some even volunteered to come to serve, to help in such things as digging the tunnel, plastering walls, and working in the kitchen. I had never thought so many brothers and sisters would come, nor that there would be so many inter-marriages between Chinese and Americans, as well as between Chinese and Japanese. From a human viewpoint, I did not like it because I felt some were married too quickly. However, on the other hand, I thought that this may be the Lord's will for the purpose of mingling everyone together. First Corinthians 12:18 says, "But now God has placed the members, each one of them, in the body, even as He willed." Right now we are all placed here. Also, verse 24 says, "God has tempered the body together." Not only did God place us together, but He also tempered us together. All that God has done is for obtaining a Body.

BROADENING OUR VIEW

When we look back to see the two thousand years of history, we feel that it is very meaningful. Before the Lord Jesus was born, God caused the Roman Empire to be raised up so that many of the prophecies in the Bible could be fulfilled. Both the Lord's birth and His death were related to the raising up of the Roman Empire. If there had been no Roman Empire, the Lord would not have been born in Bethlehem and yet have grown up in Nazareth. If the Lord had not been born during the age of the Roman Empire, He would not have been crucified, because the Jewish people did not have this kind of death sentence. Not only so, God also connected all the regions around the Mediterranean Sea together through the Roman Empire repairing the highway from Rome to Palestine. There was also the aspect of language, in that Greek became the common written and spoken language. It was after all these things were prepared that Paul came out to preach the gospel.

When Paul came out to preach the gospel, he was not in Judea. Rather, he traveled around the Mediterranean Sea with a broad view. This was why in his Epistles he said that in this new man, "There cannot be Greek and Jew, circumcision and uncircumcision, barbarian, Scythian, slave, freeman, but Christ is all and in all" (Col. 3:11). In those days, there were these problems among different groups of people. But in the new man, these differences do not exist. In the new man, everything is Christ.

Today, after two thousand years, God has brought this world to a blended stage so that there are almost no distinctions between East and West. Taiwan has large quantities of goods made in the United States, and the United States also has large quantities of goods made in Taiwan. Both the East and West are blended together. Today, if you want to be a Christian, you cannot be merely a Chinese Christian. Even the more, especially today in taking the way of the recovery, we cannot be like that. We must broaden our view. Today the Lord desires to have His Body. It does not matter whether you are willing or not; He simply likes to group all of us together. Therefore, we all have to see that the former era has already passed. From now on, the broader our view, the better.

PRACTICING TO MINGLE WITH OTHERS

Since we have seen the vision of the Body of Christ, we

need to have our practice according to this vision. We need to start practicing in small areas by first mingling with the brothers and sisters next to us. I can testify to you that I love brothers and sisters of every kind. I love those who are quick, and I also love those who are slow. I love those who are compatible with me; and I love even the more those who are not compatible with me. In these days we are translating the Chinese Recovery Version of the New Testament. Although I am more than eighty years old, I am a quick-tempered and aggressive person. Nearly all my helpers are around thirty years of age. From my viewpoint, every one of them is slow-motioned, making it necessary for me to pull them along. I do not like their slowness. It seems that many times I should have been upset, but I could not be. I said to myself, "These people are all slow-motioned. To press them to be as fast as you is an impossible task. You have to accommodate them." Therefore I am learning to be slower, accompanying them to read slowly. This does not mean that I have been affected by them. This is mingling.

The experience of those on the gospel teams is the same in principle. Some are quick-tempered, and some are slow-motioned. A slow one says, "Please wait for me. I have forgotten my small notebook." After a while he says again, "I have forgotten my *Life Lessons*." This really becomes unbearable to the quick-tempered ones. Some simply want to be quick. Only being quick can satisfy them. Eventually the quick ones end up together. Then the slow ones do not approve of the quick ones and consider that their flesh is not yet dealt with, that they are unable to bear with others or wait for others. Hence, the slow ones also end up together. Actually, to be either quick or slow is inborn; it is not up to you.

When I was a student, I was a member of the school soccer team. Some students who were very skillful liked to show off their skills when they got the ball. They dribbled the ball back and forth, not shooting for the goal right away. I was angry when I saw that because I was not there to play with the ball, but to shoot for the goal and score. Once I got the ball, I quickly kicked it into the goal. It is the same in the Lord's work today. Some very capable co-workers, once the ball of the work gets into their hands, begin playing with the ball. They do not care for the edification of the believers, nor for people's salvation. They only care to do the things that interest them. Some people feel that Bible study is very enjoyable. They start doing that and forget about the work. Some do not care for Bible studies; as long as they can get people saved, everything will be all right. There is definitely such a situation among us. Our inborn temperaments and characters are simply not the same. There are a few hundred people here, yet no two faces are the same. Even with twins, there are still differences. Our God is really capable. He created each one with a different face, and He gave a different appearance to each one.

THE BETTER THE MINGLING, THE MORE THE BLESSING

What God is doing today is to obtain the Body of Christ, not merely you as an individual, nor merely the church in a locality, nor merely the church in a country. He wants to obtain the church in the entire universe. Since this is the case, in our church life today we need to be mingled with all the brothers and sisters on the earth. The more successful the mingling, the better it is. Whoever cannot be mingled with others will eventually be disqualified by the age. In today's age, you cannot be an isolated Christian.

I have to congratulate all of you who came to the training center because it is impossible for you to get so much mingling in any other place. I wish that each one of you could come to stay in the training center for one hundred twenty days and be burned by the fire of the training center. If you do not have the grace, the light, or this vision of the Body, then the training center is a place of suffering to you. However, if you have the vision, then the training center is not only a place for training you, but also a place for perfecting you.

I hope that you can understand, receive, and at the same time, broaden your view. I am not exhorting you to be patient, to condescend, to humble yourself, or to love others as yourself. Those things are trite expressions. Rather, it is my desire that you see the light, broaden your view, and realize that we are in God's eternal economy, that you would allow God to have the Body of Christ on the earth. From now on, not only are we who are in Taipei in one accord, but the entire recovery of the Lord in the whole universe is also one. We are the one Body of Christ. Concerning this point, I have had very clear light all along. In the past three years in Taiwan, I also have gained a considerable amount of experience and realization. In these three years, the Lord has definitely done something in our midst that has broadened us. Everyone's view has been broadened. It is not enough for us merely to have a local view, nor is it enough to have an international view. We must have a universal view. We need to see that Christ is after a Body, and God will prepare a Body for Christ.

A message given by Brother Witness Lee in Taipei on September 1, 1987.

CHAPTER SIX

THE VISION OF THE BODY OF CHRIST

(2)

Scripture Reading: Eph. 1:13, 23; 2:16; 3:6

THE HOLY SPIRIT AS THE SEAL
PRODUCING THE BODY OF CHRIST

Ephesians is a book concerning the Body of Christ. Chapter one shows us God's eternal plan, that is, God's economy, from the heavens, and from eternity past. In God's economy, first, it is God the Father who has chosen us that we should be holy and without blemish. He has also predestinated us to obtain the sonship, that is, to share the life and position of His Son (1:4-5). Second, it is God the Son who came to accomplish redemption according to the selection and predestination of God the Father. Then, it is God the Spirit who applies to us and seals within us what God the Son has accomplished according to the selection and predestination of God the Father.

The Holy Spirit being the seal means that, at the time of our believing, the Holy Spirit applies within us the seal, which is constituted of what God the Father is and what God the Son is, plus what God the Father has done, that is, His selection and predestination, along with the redemption that God the Son has accomplished, plus God the Spirit Himself. The Holy Spirit applies this Triune God with all He is, all He has done, all He has attained, and all He has accomplished, as a seal within us so that all these can become our possession. Included within this possession are divinity, humanity, and the processes He has gone through, that is, His incarnation, human living, crucifixion, resurrection, and ascension.

This seal is like an all-inclusive dose which contains many different elements with different kinds of effectiveness. It is not only able to kill germs and remove the uncleanness, but also able to supply all the life elements needed by the body. When this seal is applied within us, the death of Christ becomes effective within us, killing our natural-ness, our flesh, our old creation, and our self. This seal also supplies within us the needed elements of the Spirit, with all the positive things. This sealing of the Holy Spirit as the seal within us is not a once-for-all matter, but a daily, unceasing sealing until the day of the redemption of our bodies (Eph. 4:30). The redemption of our bodies implies that the Holy Spirit will have eliminated all the things within us that are of our natural constitution, of our self, of our flesh, and of our old creation, and will have sealed within us all the elements of the Triune God, having saturated and transformed our bodies. Regeneration is the beginning of the sealing of the Holy Spirit, transformation is the continuation of this sealing, and glorification is the completion of this sealing. Our glorification through the sealing of the Holy Spirit is in reality the glory of God saturating and permeating our entire being from within. Therefore, the sealing in Ephesians chapter one includes regeneration, transformation, filling, transfusion, satura-tion, and glorification. This sealing is a slow process. It may be likened to a doctor's dispensing of medication and nourishment into a patient by injecting it into his bloodstream, thus transfusing it into every part of the patient's body so that the patient is eventually healed, becomes strong, and is transformed. The Holy Spirit is carrying out this work of transfusion within us day by day; even at the time we lose our temper, He does not stop. This is the sealing in Ephesians chapter one. The result of this sealing is that the contents and elements of the Triune God with all that He has accomplished are transfused into us.

Although in Ephesians chapter one we cannot find such terms as regeneration, filling, or transformation, yet we are shown what is the surpassing greatness of His power toward us who believe, according to the operation of the might of His strength (v. 19). First, this power raised

Christ from among the dead. This proves the greatness of this power. This is like a seed that falls into the earth and dies. For it to grow up from the earth, it must have the power of resurrection. Second, this power caused Christ to ascend to the heavens. Just for mankind to land on the moon required the expenditure of a tremendous effort. For Christ to ascend to the third heaven, the highest place in the universe, how great a power was required! Third, this power has subjected all things under Christ's feet. Fourth, this power caused Christ to be Head over all things to the church. This power operates in us with the result that the church may become the Body of Christ. The Body of Christ in Ephesians 1:23 is produced in this way. This is the first scene in the book of Ephesians concerning the vision of the Body of Christ.

This morning you should have a clear impression concerning how the Body of Christ is produced. In God's economy, this great seal of the Holy Spirit came into being after the process of God's selection and predestination and after Christ's redemption. In this seal are the all-inclusive contents of the Triune God for the dispensing of these contents into us. This seal is living. It is living within us and saturating us all the time so that all that Christ is, all He has done, and all He has attained and obtained can be sealed within us. This is how the church is produced.

This church, the Body of Christ, is unique in the universe. She is the Lord's own Body, the Father's dwelling place, the gathering of the called ones, God blended with man's race (see *Hymns*, #824). The Body of Christ in Ephesians 1:23 is the mingling of God and man. The all-inclusive, processed Triune God is mingled with the God-created, regenerated, transformed, conformed, and glorified tripartite man. This is the Body of Christ.

I believe that all the truths the Lord has released among us will one day be known by all the saved ones of God. In the Lord's recovery, we are not merely helping you trainees go out to knock on doors, preach the gospel, and baptize people. These things need to be done. The goal, however, is that you will release the truths the Lord has shown us all these years. What I am concerned about today in your going out to knock on doors, preaching the gospel, and setting up home meetings, is what kind of home meetings are actually being set up. What are the contents of the home meetings? There are differences between one home meeting that is set up and another. This altogether depends on your knowledge of the truths. You need to know Christ, and you also need to know the church. I really hope that we can see more people saved and more home meetings set up. But the home meetings need to have solid contents in order to reach our goal. I really desire to have three or four years of time to be with you week after week, so that you can obtain the transfusion of the truths. After such a time, when you go out again, you will definitely be full of the riches of Christ and be able to supply people with the riches of the truths.

RECONCILED TO GOD IN THE BODY OF CHRIST

Ephesians is a book on the Body of Christ. Ephesians chapter one shows us how the church is produced, and Ephesians chapter two shows us what kind of people these were originally who have now become the glorious Body of Christ. Verse 1 of chapter two says, "And you, being dead in your offenses and sins." Before we were saved, we were a group of walking corpses living in sins, having no feeling toward sins whatsoever. At that time, we "walked according to the age of this world, according to the ruler of the authority of the air, ... we all behaved ourselves once in the lusts of our flesh, doing the desires of the flesh and of the thoughts, and were by nature children of wrath, even as the rest" (vv. 2-3). However, because of the great love of God, one day we were saved. We were made alive from the dead. The salvation in Ephesians chapter two is different from that in the realization of many Christians, that after we believe in Jesus, God is gracious to us and saves us so that we will not go to hell, but go to heaven. Instead, the salvation here causes us to be made alive, and also to be resurrected together with Christ and seated together with Him in the

third heaven. Ephesians does not mention forgiveness of
sins here, but it mentions resurrection from the dead
because this portion is not dealing with the problem of
sins, but with the problem of death. Being raised from the
dead, having been resurrected, having ascended to the
heavens, and being seated in the heavenlies are what
Christ has accomplished through death, resurrection, and
ascension. It is in this accomplishment that the Lord
causes us who have obtained His deliverance, whether we
are Jews or Gentiles, to be made in Him a Body. We are
reconciled to God in this Body of Christ (2:16). Reconciliation with God is a matter of the Body of Christ. We are
not reconciled to God one by one individually, but we all in
one Body of Christ are once and forever reconciled to God.
Even before we were born, we and all the believers throughout the ages were reconciled to God in Christ and in
His one Body. What a revelation this is! We need to see
that even our salvation and our reconciliation to God are
matters of the Body of Christ. This is Ephesians chapter
two, showing us the second scene concerning the vision of
the Body of Christ.

ENJOYING TOGETHER THE RICHES OF CHRIST IN THE BODY OF CHRIST

Ephesians 3:6-10 shows us four important terms: the
Body (v. 6), grace (v. 8), the riches of Christ (v. 8), and the
church (v. 10). Ephesians chapter one speaks of deliverance
from sins, chapter two speaks of deliverance from death,
and chapter three speaks of grace. Grace is the unsearchable riches of Christ. This is the grace Paul obtained; this
is also the grace he preached. He obtained the riches of
Christ, and he also preached the riches of Christ. As a
result, the church was produced. This portion in Ephesians
chapter three tells us that the church which was produced
out of the riches of Christ as grace is the Body of Christ in
which you and I both have a share. This portion of the
Word also shows us that not only have we been delivered
from sin and death, on the negative side, but also, on the
positive side, we have entered into the grace of God, which

is the riches of Christ. In this grace, according to 3:6, we have become one Body, enjoying together the riches of Christ. Here sin is over, and death is eliminated. We can be in the riches of Christ, enjoying these riches as grace.

Ephesians 3:6 says, "Joint heirs and a joint Body and joint partakers of the promise." This phrase shows that the Body of Christ is a living organism which inherits the promise and receives the inheritance. According to the context, this inheritance is the riches of Christ, and these riches of Christ are the grace. Therefore, this Body of Christ is a living organism which enjoys the riches of Christ. We all are in it enjoying together the riches of Christ. This enjoyment is not an individual enjoyment, but a corporate enjoyment. If you are not in the Body of Christ, there will be no way for you to obtain this kind of enjoyment. If you are in the Body of Christ, you can obtain and partake of this kind of enjoyment. It was not God's intention in saving us that we become people enjoying Christ individually. He wants us to be in the Body of Christ to enjoy the riches of Christ together. This enjoyment is like that of the Passover lamb that was not for individuals, but for the whole family. Every one of the Israelites needed to eat together with his whole family. No one was allowed to take his own lamb and eat by himself. Therefore, the third scene concerning the vision of the Body of Christ, in Ephesians chapter three, shows us clearly that we need to be heirs and partakers of the promise in the one Body of Christ in order to share the unsearchable riches of Christ.

A message given by Brother Witness Lee in Taipei on September 3, 1987.

CHAPTER SEVEN

THE WAY OF MEETING AS REVEALED IN THE NEW TESTAMENT

Scripture Reading: Matt. 18:20; Acts 5:42; 20:7; 1 Cor. 14:23a, 26; Heb. 10:25

I have two important burdens these days. One is what I have shared with you in the past concerning the vision of the Body of Christ; the other is what I am going to share with you now concerning the way of meeting as revealed in the New Testament. This is the burden which has been in me for the past three years.

THE NEED TO CHANGE THE SYSTEM OF MEETINGS

Three years ago when I returned to Taipei, I brought up the matter of changing the system. We need to change the system of meetings. Now we have had more than three years of preparation. I feel that the church in Taipei should give this matter a thorough review. It may be that after another month we will have a thorough rearrangement of the way of our meetings. This is something unprecedented, not only among ourselves, but also within the twenty-century-old Christianity. We need to go back to the apostolic age to receive and carry on the way of meeting as it was when the apostles were on earth.

At present, among the different halls of the church in Taipei, there are about thirty-five hundred in the meeting on the Lord's Day. If we include everyone who comes to meet at different times, the number is about five thousand. In addition, in the trainings held for the past two years, there have been about twenty-six to twenty-seven thousand people gained through door knocking. Less than one quarter, about five thousand, have remained to meet with us in the districts. If we add these two categories together, the old and the new ones, the church in Taipei has about ten thousand people who come to meet at different times. This situation is merely a transition. This transitional period has been long enough, however, and I feel this is the time we should have a major rearrangement.

Moreover, in considering again and again before the Lord in the last few days, I feel that the believers, not only the newly saved ones but also those who have been saved for years, are not clear concerning the way of the believers' meetings. I am afraid that even among the co-workers and elders, there are not many who thoroughly understand. Therefore, I would like to give you some suggestions concerning this matter. I hope that you will write these down point by point so that after you have gone home, you can study thoroughly what is the proper way of meeting for the believers according to the divine revelation in the New Testament. Then we will study further how to practice this way of meeting. If we merely see a way and do not know how to practice it, we are still outsiders having no way to enter in.

NOT FOLLOWING THE CUSTOMS OF THE NATIONS

In 1933, for the first time I went to Shanghai, which was the place where Brother Nee was working. In that place was the largest church, the leading church in the whole of China at that time. After a certain time, I heard Brother Nee say that the way of meeting we were practicing was following the customs of degraded Christianity; it was not according to God's desire nor according to the Bible. He cited the words of the type in the Old Testament in Leviticus 20:23: "Ye shall not walk in the manners of the nations, which I cast out before you: for they committed all these things, and therefore I abhorred them." He said that the whole system of meetings in Christianity today is the customs of the nations. The nations he spoke of were not the Gentile nations in the New Testament age today; rather, he referred to the many denominations of the deformed Christianity. These many denominations are the denominated assemblies in Christianity. They are typified in the Old Testament by the nations that became problems to the Israelites. After hearing Brother Nee's word that day, for the past fifty years we have been trying to eliminate this thing from among us. Nevertheless, not only have we not eliminated it, but we have unintentionally strengthened it.

From the time Brother Nee saw the error of the customs of the denominations, he began to condemn the system of meetings at that time and also endeavored to find out from the Bible the way of meeting for the believers. He also spent time to study the practices of the various denominations. Until his departure from the earth, however, he had not found a way to practice. This brother who brought the Lord's recovery into our midst saw clearly fifty-four years ago that, although we had left Christianity, the customs of the nations as seen in the meetings of Christianity were still following us. We have not yet eliminated this thing; even until this morning, we have not been fully freed from it. I would like to speak a frank word to you trainees, especially those who have received training for the past two terms and are now in the communities concentrating on home meetings, small group meetings, and district meetings. I am very concerned for those meetings in which you are serving, whether they are totally according to the new way, or are partly old and partly new. How do you actually carry out the meetings? What do you do? What kind of results have you produced? We should know that in anything we do, the natural way is very simple. But if you have to work by absolutely following instructions, then it is not so easy. I am afraid that after all you have done, it is still the same way, the old way. Therefore, I would like to remind you and also offer you some materials for further study.

THE PROPER WAY OF MEETING FOR BELIEVERS

Concerning the proper way of meeting for believers, there are five passages in the New Testament that are the strongest and can afford us the practical help. The first passage is Matthew 18:20. Here the Lord said, "For where two or three are gathered together in My name, there I am in their midst." This is the first time the Bible speaks about the meeting of the believers. The Lord mentioned only two or three. This is what we call a small group meeting. The second passage is Acts 5:42. Here it says, "And every day, in the temple and from house to house, they did not cease teaching and bringing the good news of Jesus as the Christ." On the day of Pentecost, three thousand were saved. Not only did they have a large gathering in the temple, but they also had small meetings in people's homes. Every household was preaching the gospel, speaking the teachings of the apostles, bringing people to know Christ and pursue after Christ, having the breaking of bread to remember the Lord, and having prayers.

The third passage is Acts 20:7 where it says that when Paul was staying in Troas for seven days, on the first day of the week they gathered together to break bread. Because Paul had to start his journey the next day, he spoke to them even until midnight. After the breaking of bread, he conversed again with the believers for a considerable time (v. 11). This must have been the meeting for the whole church in Troas rather than a small group meeting.

The fourth passage is 1 Corinthians 14:23, where it says, "If...the whole church comes together in one place." Although the New Testament shows us from the beginning that the meeting of the believers was based on small groups and homes, yet here in 1 Corinthians 14 it tells us that sometimes the whole church also gathers together. Verse 26 continues, "What is it then, brothers? Whenever you come together, each one has a psalm, has a teaching, has a revelation, has a tongue, has an interpretation. Let all things be done for building up." Therefore, the church meets regularly in homes and in small groups. Sometimes the believers also need to come together, not to listen to one speaker, but to allow everyone to function, for each one to present his portion of supply.

The last passage is Hebrews 10:25 where it says, "Not forsaking the assembling of ourselves together, as the custom with some is, but exhorting one another." This word was spoken to the Hebrew believers who were originally in Judaism and had Judaic meetings. Now that they had become Christians, they had their own meetings, which were the church meetings. These church meetings, regardless of whether they are small group meetings or large gatherings, are not one-sided, with one person speaking and the rest listening, but mutual, with each one exhorting the others.

NOT ONE-SIDED, BUT MUTUAL

These five portions of the Scriptures show us definitely the way of meeting for the New Testament believers. First, the basic meetings are home meetings and small group meetings. Second, as needed, the whole church may gather together. Third, regardless of whether it is a home meeting, a small group meeting, or a large meeting, it is absolutely not a one-sided speaking, but speaking in mutuality and with one another. When the Apostle Paul spoke concerning the whole church coming together, he even used the expression "each one." This shows that each one should have a supply, and each one can have a supply. This is the principle of the believers' meeting. This principle completely nullifies the existing way of meeting practiced by every denomination and sect in Christianity. Some of you were in Christianity and clearly know the situation among them. Was there a time when the pastor and the congregation spoke mutually? It has always been the pastor alone speaking and the congregation listening. From the viewpoint of history, people like to have only large gatherings, which are usually one-sided, with one person speaking and the rest listening. This is the practice of the nations. The meeting of the believers, however, is not like this; it is with mutuality and speaking one to another. Only by taking this way can we be delivered from the way of meeting of the nations. Otherwise, we are merely following the customs of the nations. It is not that we did not see this light in the past. We did see it, but we did not know how to practice it; therefore, we did not make a special effort to carry it out. For this reason, until today the meetings are still one-sided, for the most part, and short of mutuality. The way of meeting by following the customs of the nations to speak in a one-sided way is absolutely natural. When people attend such meetings, they always wait to listen to others. No one has the thought that they need to speak. Even if they would like to speak, they do not know what to speak and do not have the boldness to speak.

CHRISTIANITY HAVING CHOKED TO DEATH THE FUNCTIONS OF THE SAINTS

In today's age, people cannot do without religion. In the minds of most people, the highest and most genuine religion is Christianity because Christianity worships the true God and also because the Bible is the most superior book. Moreover, there are the Sunday services. When people come into a chapel for the Sunday services, they feel calm and peaceful, with everything in order. After taking their seats in the midst and listening to the choir singing in harmony, they really feel soothed. After that, there is Bible reading for the sermon, with the pastor leading the congregation in prayer. Then another pastor gives a sermon, and finally, the resident pastor gives the benediction. After the meeting, these pastors and preachers will even go to the door to greet the people as they leave. Would you not say that this kind of service is good? If I were short of spiritual enlightenment, I would definitely choose such a chapel. This practice matches the psychology of the congregation and is very much welcomed by people. But such practices have completely choked to death the functions of the truly saved ones. Because the functions of the believers have all been choked to death, the only thing they can do is to send away those who have the desire to become preachers to be educated in seminaries, expecting that after graduation they will consecrate themselves to be preachers or pastors to maintain the Sunday morning services in the various chapels. Hence, they will become the clergymen. With this kind of clergy-laity system, there is absolutely no way for the Lord to carry out His New Testament economy for the building up of the Body of Christ.

THE PROPER WAY TO PRACTICE MEETING

The way revealed in the New Testament is exactly opposite to what we have described. Once a person has believed in the Lord and is saved, the first thing we do is to help him pray, call on the name of the Lord, and sing hymns to praise the Lord. The next thing is to lead him to practice speaking, testifying for the Lord. After that, we lead him to meet together with his family members, and with his neighbors and relatives, to speak Jesus to them. He has no knowledge whatever that there are the so-called pastors or preachers. At the present, the practice among us is a combination of the old and the new way. Because we have remained in this way for too long, we are accustomed to the customs of the nations. Hence, once we change the system of meeting from one person speaking to many speaking, some brothers and sisters are not accustomed to such a thing, and they will not necessarily like it. This is our problem. What should we do? If we want to keep the way of meeting as revealed in the New Testament, then we must exercise ourselves in every meeting. How we entered the door should also be the way we walk. Since we were saved through calling on the name of the Lord, then after being saved, we should be those who call on the name of the Lord and speak to the Lord whenever we meet. We should do this even on the way to the meeting, before we arrive. Then we will speak, testify, and preach Jesus to others in the meetings, or we will pray and praise. Whoever comes to the meeting, regardless of who he is, should practice in this way. It should not be something done once in a while, but in every meeting.

STUDYING TOGETHER HOW TO IMPROVE IN THE MATTERS OF THE WORD, THE SPIRIT, PRAYING, AND SINGING

There is another vital point about the meetings as revealed in the New Testament; that is, in these meetings, first, there needs to be the word. Everyone should speak the word of God. Second, there needs to be the Spirit. Everyone should exercise the spirit and be living. Third, there needs to be prayer. Fourth, there needs to be singing. These four items, the word, the Spirit, praying, and singing, should be the content of our meetings. The reason our home meetings and small group meetings are not good is that the word is not spoken properly, the spirit is not released, the prayer is poor, and singing is lacking. If these four matters are not carried out properly, our meetings will be finished, and no one will want to come again.

From now on, I beg you trainees and the trainers as well to have more study on how to improve in the matters of the word, the Spirit, praying, and singing as revealed in the Bible. I myself also will study. In the past twenty years, the Lord has led us to practice pray-reading, and we have been helped greatly. Recently, we have had the propagation groups here enjoying the Lord through pray-reading, and the benefits are not small. At any rate, in the meetings of the believers, whether they are home meetings, small group meetings, or large meetings, it is worthwhile for us to study how to practice these four things—the word, the Spirit, praying, and singing—through pray-reading and the propagation groups. I would ask that you bring these points back home and study them thoroughly. May the Lord bless you and bless us. These days are really days of warfare. I hope that some of you would pick up the burden of offering fighting prayers to ward off the enemy's frustrations. May the Lord have mercy on us.

A message given by Brother Witness Lee in Taipei on October 6, 1987.

Chapter Eight

THE KEY
TO THE NEW TESTAMENT MEETINGS—
BEING FILLED IN THE SPIRIT
WITH THE TRIUNE GOD

Scripture Reading: Eph. 5:18-20; John 14:23; Eph. 3:19; Acts 13:52

In the last chapter we considered the way of meeting as revealed in the New Testament, and we described its general outline. This morning, we need to continue to point out the key to the New Testament meetings.

THE LAW BEING THE CENTER
OF THE OLD TESTAMENT MEETINGS

The Bible reveals to us that in the Old Testament it was after the children of Israel were called out of Egypt that God began to require them to have meetings. Before this time, from Adam through the patriarchs including Abel, Enosh, Enoch, Noah, Abraham, Isaac, and Jacob, there had been no such problem as meetings. It was not until the Israelites had become a nation, had fallen into Egypt, and were rescued by God to the wilderness, that God began to teach them how to meet. At that time, God gave them the law so that they would take the law as their center. Every time they met, they would emphasize teaching the law and expounding the law. As long as they could be clear and accurate concerning the law, they would have no problems before God. Therefore, the Old Testament meetings were altogether a matter of the letter and of knowledge.

THE HOLY SPIRIT BEING THE CENTER
OF THE NEW TESTAMENT MEETINGS

In the New Testament, God's economy has overthrown everything of the Old Testament. God does not want the law to be the center of His people's meetings any longer, but rather He wants His Spirit to be the center. The meetings are not of the letter, but of life; they are not of knowledge, but of reality. Because the New Testament meetings have the Spirit of God as the center, they are of life and of reality. Such meetings could not possibly be carried out by the practice of one person speaking and the rest listening. If the meeting is a matter of the letter and of knowledge, there is a need for someone who can understand, apprehend, and comprehend, like a lawyer. When that person speaks and everyone understands, the job is accomplished. In the New Testament age, however, the meeting is entirely a matter of the Spirit. Therefore, it is not sufficient to have only speaking and teaching.

I repeat, the Old Testament meetings centered around the law, which was entirely of the letter and of knowledge. The New Testament meetings center around the Holy Spirit, who is of life and of reality. In the Old Testament times, as long as there was a lawyer who understood the law, such as Ezra, he could gather the people together and expound the law clearly to them. This was merely a teaching of the letter so that the people could obtain the knowledge of the letter. In the New Testament, the Holy Spirit replaces the law. The Holy Spirit is not the letter, but life; He is not knowledge, but reality. This Holy Spirit is the transfiguration of Christ, and He is simply Christ Himself. And Christ is the embodiment of God. Therefore, the Holy Spirit is the Triune God. This Triune God has been manifested to us and has reached us, and even has entered into us to indwell us to be our life and our person. The Holy Spirit is the ultimate expression of the Triune God, who eventually enters into us to mingle as one with His redeemed and regenerated people so that we and He, He and we, can become one. This is the greatest mystery in the universe. The New Testament meetings are concerned with this.

Some of you brothers and sisters here were born in Christianity and were Christians there, some were born among us and have grown up in the churches of the

Lord's recovery, and some were Gentiles originally who were saved and came into the churches of the Lord's recovery. Regardless of which kind of background you came from, I believe that before this time you had no understanding concerning the simple statements I just made regarding the believers' meetings. Therefore, I would like to give you some basic training concerning this point. You need to realize that we are in the midst of a change of the system in the church. I have a very heavy burden to present to you trainees the basic issues of the change of the system in a clear and understandable way. I hope that while I am in your midst taking the lead in this training, the Lord will have mercy on me to make me a qualified "doctor" so that I can diagnose your real problems thoroughly. I would like to speak an honest word. Today there are still many Christians who may have read the Bible for years, pursued the Lord diligently, or studied theology, and yet may nevertheless have difficulty pointing out what were the meetings among God's people in the Old Testament, and again what are the meetings among God's people in the New Testament. But this morning, after so much experience, so much study, and so much consideration, I can stand before you to tell you in simple words that the meetings of God's people in the Old Testament were of the law, of the letter, and of knowledge; the meetings of us believers in the New Testament are of the Holy Spirit, of life, and of reality.

I would like to speak a little more lest you do not understand. For example, there is the matter of redemption in the Bible. In the Old Testament, however, there was only the knowledge of redemption without the reality, because at that time redemption had not been accomplished yet. In the New Testament, whenever we meet together, not only do we have the knowledge of redemption, but we also have its reality. Not only do we preach the doctrine of redemption, but we also teach this matter of redemption and help people to be redeemed. In the Old Testament, even if people wanted to be redeemed, they could not be redeemed because redemption had not yet been accomplished. At most, they could only have the knowledge of redemption and the type of redemption, which was merely a shadow.

THE NEW TESTAMENT MEETING NOT REQUIRING TEACHING, BUT REQUIRING TRANSMISSION

Because the meetings of the Old Testament were of the law, of the letter, and of knowledge, there was a need for teaching, just like people attending schools need to be taught. However, since the meetings of the New Testament are of the Holy Spirit, of life, and of reality, strictly speaking, there is no need of teaching. This is clearly pointed out in the New Testament. First, Hebrews chapter eight tells us that God has put His new covenant, which is the law of life, in us so that we would know the Lord and would not need the teaching of the outward letter. Second, 1 John chapter two shows us that we have received the anointing from the Lord. This anointing abides in us, and we do not need other people to teach us. The anointing teaches us in all things. From this you can see that the New Testament meeting does not require teachings.

Although the New Testament meeting does not require teachings, it requires transmission. For example, the meeting place here is very hot now, and we need air conditioning. Suppose we invite a brother to teach us about air conditioning. We may not have felt uncomfortably hot before he spoke, but the more he talks, on the contrary, the hotter we feel. Before he has spoken for half an hour, we have become so hot that we cannot tolerate it any longer. We will all say, "We do not want you to teach us about air conditioning; we want air conditioning." What should we do? We simply need to locate the switch for the air conditioner and switch on the power source. Once the electricity is transmitted and the motor is turned, the cool air comes out. Degraded Christianity has made the serious mistake of returning to the Old Testament from the New

Testament, so that among them they nearly have only teachings with no transmission or infusion. To some extent, among us we have also committed the same mistake.

BEING FILLED IN SPIRIT, RECITING HYMNS, OVERFLOWING WITH PRAISES

We need to know that the key to the New Testament meetings is with the Holy Spirit. The Holy Spirit is the Triune God. He is not at all objective to us. He is not only in the heavens, nor only present with us saved ones; He has entered into us. To speak of this matter, the New Testament uses a word that was not used in this sense in the Old Testament. This word is "filling." The Holy Spirit, who is God Himself, not only enters into us, but also fills us. This is not a small matter. Where is God filling us? It is not in our mind but in our spirit. Therefore, Ephesians 5:18 tells us that we should be filled in spirit. According to the revelation of the entire book of Ephesians, to be filled in spirit is to be filled with the Triune God. The Triune God will fill us to such an extent that even the Father and the Son will come to make home in us (John 14:23). Ephesians 3:17 also says that Christ the Son is not only in our spirit, but even the more, He wants to make home in our hearts. Acts 13:52 says that the disciples were all filled with joy and with the Holy Spirit.

When we put these verses together, we can see that the Triune God—God the Father, God the Son, and God the Spirit—desires to make home in us and indwell us to become our inward joy and completely fill our whole being. The result of such a filling is what is mentioned in Ephesians 5:19, "Speaking to one another in psalms and hymns and spiritual songs, singing and psalming with your heart to the Lord." Therefore, the result of being filled with the Holy Spirit is to overflow with words of praise. The psalms, hymns, and spiritual songs referred to here by the Apostle Paul are not ordinary words. Therefore, we all need to learn. Recently, I heard that some of you are memorizing Bible verses. I hope that you would also memorize hymns. For example, consider the words from *Hymns*, #397:

> More gratitude give me,
> More trust in the Lord,
> More zeal for His glory,
> More hope in His Word,
> More tears for His sorrows,
> More pain at His grief,
> More meekness in trial,
> More praise for relief.

If these words are thoroughly memorized within you, when you are filled in spirit and moved by the Spirit, you will spontaneously sing out, "More gratitude give me, More trust in the Lord...." Sometimes you may not necessarily sing all three stanzas. It may be that you will sing only the last stanza and think of the Lord's return:

> More victory give me,
> More strength to o'ercome,
> More freedom from earth-stains,
> More quest for the throne,
> More fit for the Kingdom....

From this point of view, the hymns are more useful than the Bible verses. Another example is *Hymns*, #717:

> O let us rejoice in the Lord evermore,
> Though all things around us be trying,
> Though floods of affliction like sea billows roar,
> It's better to sing than be sighing.
>
> > Then rejoice evermore, rejoice evermore,
> > It is better to sing than be sighing:
> > It is better to live than be dying;
> > So let us rejoice evermore.

Once you sing like this, your coldness will turn to zeal, your deadness will turn to life, your weakness will turn to strength, and your sorrow will turn to joy. Therefore, you should memorize the hymns thoroughly. At the same time, you need to be filled within. If there is no filling, there will be no overflow.

Here is another hymn we should also sing:

> Hallelujah! Christ is Victor,
>   Tell with every breath,
> That the Savior still is conqu'ror
>   Over sin and death.
>
>> Hallelujah! Christ is Victor,
>>   Tell where'er you go,
>> That the Lord is still the conqu'ror,
>>   Over every foe.
>>   (*Hymns,* #890, stanza 1)

When I have a little sickness, I like to sing the second stanza the most:

> Hallelujah! Christ is Victor,
>   Pain and sickness flee,
> When we plead the mighty victory
>   Won on Calvary.

The fourth stanza is also very good:

> Hallelujah! Christ is Victor,
>   No defeat nor fear
> Evermore must dim thy vision!
>   Christ the way will clear.

I am one who does not know how to sing, but I love to sing hymns. First, I sing to myself; second, I sing to the angels; and third, I sing to the demons surrounding me. I would like to sing again:

> O let us rejoice in the Lord evermore,
> When sickness upon us is stealing,
> No cordial like gladness our strength can restore,
> For joy is the fountain of healing.
>   (*Hymns,* #717, stanza 3)

This is indeed wonderful! It is good to memorize Bible verses; nevertheless, by that memorization alone, we simply cannot get the taste that we have with singing and praising.

PERSONAL REVIVAL AND
HOUSE-TO-HOUSE PROPAGATION

When we are filled in spirit, full of the Spirit, the four major factors for our meetings—the word, the Spirit, singing, and praying—will all become useful. These four major factors are related to the Spirit. Without the Spirit, the word is dead. Without the Spirit, the singing and the praying are also dead. All of our singing should overflow from the spirit and be sung from the spirit. We should sing by being filled with the Spirit:

> Hallelujah! Hallelujah!
> I have passed the riven veil,
> Here the glories never fail,
> Hallelujah! Hallelujah!
> I am living in the presence of the King.
> (*Hymns,* #551, chorus)

At any rate, we must be living persons, filled with the Holy Spirit, in order to be qualified to have Christian meetings. Due to the degraded system of meeting, Christianity has caused all the Sunday-goers to become either dead or sick or paralyzed in their spirit. If they are asked to speak, they do not have any words to say. If they are asked to praise, they feel that it would be as hard as going to heaven. Some brothers and sisters among us are also like this. When they come to the meeting, if they are asked to function according to 1 Corinthians 14:26, "Each one has a psalm, has a teaching, has a revelation," it would be impossible.

For this reason, I said to you two months ago that the first thing each one of you should do when you wake up in the morning is to call: "O Lord Jesus!" The second thing is that you should open the Bible to have fellowship with the Lord using two verses. You should get yourself enlivened through reading and then live Christ in the spirit all day long. In the evening, you may either have a home meeting with your own family members, or have a small group meeting with the neighboring brothers and sisters, or attend a district meeting or a meeting at the hall; in any case, your spirit should be living. This makes it necessary for us to have a basic revival—to be living persons and to live a life that is living. Not only should we have fellowship with the Lord and have home meetings, but we also need to develop to the point where we have small group meetings, and then, even further, propagation groups. Only in this way can the church have the spreading and increase. This is the kind of meeting the Lord is after, as revealed in the Bible, and it is what we should have.

I remember that the meetings in Elden Hall of Los Angeles during 1969 and 1970 were just like this. The brothers and sisters regularly enjoyed the Lord in the homes all day long and sang hymns. They would sing on their way to the meeting, and everyone was living. Whoever came to the meeting could open his mouth and function. That kind of meeting was fully delivered from the habit of one man preaching and the others listening. Instead, everyone functioned, helping one another and edifying one another. This is my hope toward you. I hope that you all can receive this fellowship.

A message given by Brother Witness Lee in Taipei on October 8, 1987.

CHAPTER NINE

THE SIGNIFICANCE OF BEING FILLED IN THE SPIRIT WITH THE TRIUNE GOD

Scripture Reading: Eph. 5:18-19; John 3:6; 4:24; Rom. 8:16; 12:11; 2 Tim. 4:22; Matt. 10:32; John 17:21

In the preceding message, I presented to you the matter of being filled in the spirit with the Triune God. This is not a small matter. This is the key to our experience and enjoyment of Christ. The central point of God's New Testament economy is that this processed Triune God has become the all-inclusive, life-giving Spirit and come into us to mingle as one with the tripartite man. He is our life, and we are His living. This living is a living of being filled in our spirit with the Triune God. The entire New Testament takes this as the key, as the secret, as far as the revelation of our experience of the Lord is concerned.

BEING SENT BY THE TRIUNE GOD,
FILLED WITH THE TRIUNE GOD,
AND GOING OUT TO KNOCK ON DOORS
WITH THE TRIUNE GOD FOR GOSPEL PREACHING

Your going out to visit homes to contact people, bring them to salvation, dispense Christ into them, and baptize them into the Triune God who is the Father, the Son, and the Spirit, is a great matter that shakes heaven and earth. This is not a superstitious performance, but a real fact. This matter is too marvelous and too wonderful! I am afraid that even those of us who have knocked on doors to preach the gospel for a long time do not have a thorough realization regarding the matter of bringing people to believe in the Lord and baptizing them into the Triune God. If we had a thorough realization, we would feel that we have absolutely no way to carry out this matter by ourselves. We can do it because the Triune God is within us, filling us, and mingling with us as one.

Therefore, when you go to knock on doors to preach the gospel, it is not only you who are going, but the Triune God going together with you. You may say that you bring the Triune God with you to knock on doors to preach the gospel; or you may also say that the Triune God brings you with Him to knock on doors to preach the gospel. If you are clear concerning this vision, your hand will not be trembling when you knock on the doors. When someone opens the door, it is not necessary to say the same thing every time, "I am sent by such-and-such church." You may say, "The Triune God and I are coming to visit you." You may also say, "The Lord Jesus Christ wants me to come with Him to visit you." You may even speak in this way, "The ever-living God has brought me here today to visit you."

In Matthew 10:19-20, the Lord Jesus says, "But when they deliver you up...it shall be given to you in that hour what you shall speak; for you are not the ones speaking, but the Spirit of your Father is the One speaking in you." I have definitely experienced what the Lord promised here. When the Japanese were invading China, I was taken away by the Japanese twice when I was in the enemy-occupied area. One time I was confined day and night for thirty days, and was interrogated twice a day for two to three hours each time. I definitely had the experience of answering questions before the so-called government officials. I can testify that the Lord was really with me and was within me helping me to speak. One day, they brought me out of the prison and asked me, "You had revival meetings. What is the meaning of revival meetings?" I said, "Christianity always has 'stirring-up' meetings. The terms we use for all the activities in our church, however, must be scriptural. In the Bible, you cannot find such a term as 'stirring up,' but rather the term 'revival' is used." He then asked me, "Where does the Bible say revival?" I immediately replied, "Habakkuk chapter three." He tossed the Bible to me and said, "Show it to me!" The Bible has sixty-six books with more than a thousand pages. But that day I randomly opened it right to the page of Habakkuk chapter three. Further, I pointed with my finger right to the word revive! "O Lord, revive thy work in the midst of the years" (v. 2). When that official who was questioning me saw this happen, he became quiet for a period of time and was subdued. He did not know how to question me further. I believe he must have realized that there was something special with me.

We who go out to knock on doors to preach the gospel need to have this vision. We need to see that not only does the Triune God send me, but He also fills me and mingles with me, and that I and He, He and I, are one. When the sisters go out to knock on doors to preach the gospel, more or less they have some fear. You need to realize, however, that it is not you alone who are going, but the Triune God who has mingled Himself with you is going with you. When someone opens his door, you should say boldly, "The Triune God has sent me to bring Him along with me to visit you." Even though he may not understand, he can realize that there is something special coming out of you. This is like that woman with the issue of blood who touched the garment of the Lord Jesus; the Lord felt power going out of Him (Mark 5:30). You and I should have such a faith. When we go out to knock on doors to preach the gospel, once our mouths are opened and the word has gone out, power will be passed on to others from us. This is the genuine preaching of the gospel by knocking on doors.

THE PLEASURE OF THE TRIUNE GOD
BEING TO FILL THE REDEEMED

The Triune God filling the redeemed tripartite persons is a matter of His heart's pleasure. This pleasure of God is simply His desire, and it has become His will. This pleasure and desire of God then became His eternal plan, His intention, and His arrangement. Therefore, God's pleasure, will, and purpose have become His plan, intention, and arrangement. This is God's economy.

The Triune God Being Processed
to Become the Ultimately Consummated Spirit

It is according to His economy that God administrates

this plan. The first step He took was creation. When the man He had created became fallen, He took the second step, the step of redemption. This redemptive work of God has to do with the Father, the Son, and the Spirit. In eternity, the Father arranged, designed, and intended everything according to His plan. In time, at the fullness of time, the Son came to become a man, putting on man's flesh, having man's likeness and man's nature, and lived among men for thirty-three and a half years. In His human body, with a human form and with the human nature, He Himself worked, preached, performed miracles, and brought His disciples to live and move together with Him for three and a half years. Then He went to the cross, being willing to enter into death to experience death. According to the flesh, He entered into the tomb; according to the spirit and the soul, He entered into Hades and remained there for a period of three days. In Hades He displayed Himself for all the principalities of death to see, proving that He is one who cannot be held by death, but has overcome death and is resurrected. He went into death by Himself; in the same way, He came out of death by Himself. Once He came out of death and entered into resurrection, He was transfigured from the likeness of the flesh to the likeness of the Spirit. Therefore in resurrection, He became the life-giving Spirit (1 Cor. 15:45b). This life-giving Spirit is the ultimately consummated Triune God.

The Triune God Breathing Himself into the Believers

After the Lord had become the life-giving Spirit in resurrection, He came back into the midst of the disciples. John chapter twenty records that His return after resurrection was a very mysterious thing. He was the pneumatic Christ coming back with a resurrected body (Luke 24:39-40). After He came back, He breathed into the disciples, signifying that He breathed Himself into them, saying, "Receive the Holy Spirit" (John 20:22). This portion can also be translated, "Receive the Holy Breath [*pneuma*]." This was an unusual divine breath. This divine breath was God Himself. At that time, He was no longer the unprocessed God, as He had been before the thirty-three and a half years; rather, He had passed through incarnation, being conceived in a virgin's womb, and was born, and living among men, He passed through thirty-three and a half years of human life. Then He went to the cross and even entered into death and Hades, where He displayed His victory. Then He came out of death and entered into resurrection. Once He entered into resurrection, He became the Spirit who was this very breath, the holy breath.

What I am speaking to you is entirely according to the revelation of the Bible. It has taken me about thirty years to be able to speak these words in this way, with the intention of getting away from the general way of speaking in Christianity, and its influence. However, I have not at all departed from the truth. This new way of speaking is not a new revelation. I am using a new way of speaking to present to you an ancient truth that is precious. It was because of this new speaking that I have provoked people to condemn me by saying that my speaking concerning Christ as the Spirit is heresy. However, let me tell you that the truth is the truth, and eventually the truth will win the victory. In order to defend their erroneous teaching concerning the Trinity, degraded Christianity absolutely will not admit that Christ is the Spirit. They say that the Father is the Father, Christ is Christ, and the Spirit is the Spirit. Nevertheless, they have no way to annul what was definitely indicated in 1 Corinthians 15:45, which says, "The last Adam became a life-giving Spirit," and what was clearly declared in 2 Corinthians 3:17, which says, "The Lord is the Spirit."

After the Triune God had passed through all the processes, He came forth as the ultimately consummated Spirit. This ultimately consummated Spirit is the processed Triune God. This One is our God and our Father. He is also our Lord, our Savior, our Redeemer, our Master, and the Spirit as well. He is our life, and our wisdom: righteousness, sanctification, and redemption. He is even our patience, our humility, and all our virtues. He is our all in all.

ALL THE NORMAL RELATIONSHIPS
BETWEEN GOD AND MAN BEING OF THE SPIRIT

The ultimate consummation of this Triune God is the Spirit. His very nature is also the Spirit because God is Spirit (John 4:24). Not only so, the last Person of this Triune God—the Father, the Son, and the Spirit—is the Spirit. The Father is in the Son, and the Son is the Spirit. Therefore, the Triune God ultimately is the Spirit. This God, who is the Spirit and whose last Person of the Divine Trinity is also the Spirit, has passed through various processes. Moreover, He has entered into resurrection in His divinity with His humanity to become the life-giving Spirit. Therefore, the Lord in resurrection has breathed Himself as the all-inclusive Spirit into the believers. This very God in whom we believe is altogether a matter of the Spirit.

For the purpose of dispensing this Spirit into us, God in His creation of man particularly created a spirit for him that he might receive this God who is the Spirit by the spirit and with the spirit. Then, when He came back in His resurrection, the first thing He did was to enter into man's spirit to regenerate his spirit. This is spoken of as "that which is born of the Spirit is spirit" (John 3:6). This is a matter of the Spirit begetting the spirit.

If we want to worship God, we must worship Him in our regenerated spirit. This is a matter of the spirit worshipping the Spirit. Today all the relationships between man and God are in the spirit. One of the Chinese hymns contains this word: "All the normal relationships between God and man are altogether in the Spirit." The chorus says, "The Spirit begets the spirit, the spirit worships the Spirit, and eventually the Spirit will fill me."

Romans 8:16 says, "The Spirit Himself witnesses with our spirit." The Spirit witnesses with the spirit. Second Timothy 4:22 says, "The Lord be with your spirit." It does not say here that the Lord should be with our mind, or that the Lord should be with our heart. Rather, it says, "The Lord be with your spirit." This clearly shows us that our spirit is the unique place where the Lord is.

Also, Matthew 10:32 says, "Every one therefore who in Me shall confess Me before men, I also in him will confess him before My Father who is in the heavens." Here it says that our confessing of the Lord is a matter of us in Him confessing the Lord. The Lord's confessing of us is the Lord in us confessing us. This means that whenever we call on the Lord's name, we are in the Lord. As soon as we confess the Lord Jesus, we are in the spirit, and we are in Him. Our union with the Lord can reach such a degree!

Therefore, in John 15:4, the Lord said, "Abide in Me and I in you." At the end of John 17, the Lord prayed, saying, "You, Father, are in Me and I in You, that they [the disciples] also may be in Us [the Triune God]" (v. 21). Today we believers are in the Triune God. This is altogether a matter of the spirit.

TO BE FILLED WITH THE TRIUNE GOD BEING A NORMAL MATTER

In Christianity, most of the teachers consider the matter of being filled with the Spirit as a very miraculous and extraordinary thing. Fundamental Christianity does not touch this matter much. On the other hand, the Pentecostals touch this matter in an improper way; they are too wild. However, according to the Bible, God, having passed through the different processes, became the life-giving Spirit and breathed Himself into His believers, that is, into His Body. Therefore, our being filled with the Triune God is a very normal matter, as normal as our regeneration.

In the New Testament Christ came; hence, the New Testament is the age of Christ. Then Christ went through death and resurrection to become the Spirit; hence, the New Testament is also the age of the Spirit. Furthermore, the Spirit has become the word; hence, the New Testament is also the age of the word. Romans 10:8 says, "The word is near you, in your mouth and in your heart." As long as you receive any gospel word in the Bible, this word within you is Spirit, and this Spirit is simply Christ. Therefore, today it is not too difficult to be filled with the Triune God;

rather, it is a miraculous normality. Romans 10:13 says, "For, Whoever calls upon the name of the Lord shall be saved." Once you call on the name of the Lord, the Lord who is the Spirit within you will carry out His deliverance so that you may obtain salvation. Nothing can be more normal than this. When a sinner hears the gospel, he is moved to repent and call on the Lord from within, saying, "O Lord Jesus! Forgive my sins! I receive You." It is in this simple way that the Lord the Spirit comes into him. To be filled in the Spirit is just as normal as this.

PRACTICING TO BE FILLED WITH THE SPIRIT BY CALLING ON THE LORD AND SPEAKING THE LORD ALL THE DAY LONG

After we have received the Lord in this way, we need to always say, "O Lord!" You don't need to analyze whether this calling is in the spirit or not. You simply call. We all have had experiences like these. When we weep, repent, and call on the name of the Lord, we always have a very good feeling and the sense of the Lord's presence. That is the Triune God filling us. At such a time, the sense within us is that the Lord Jesus seems to be right before us; it seems that we have entered into an atmosphere that causes us to feel very sweet, satisfied, and comfortable.

Therefore, when we get up in the morning, the best thing for us to do is not to think about other things, but only to think about the Lord Jesus. It is easy to talk about this, but it is not simple to practice. This is because we all have many things filling our hearts. In spite of this, we still need to practice. There is a difference between calling on the Lord the first thing before getting out of bed, and getting out of bed without calling. You need to call on the Lord in this way in the morning. Then during the whole day, you need to practice speaking the Lord. When there is no one with you, you should call on the Lord Jesus; when there are others with you, you should speak the Lord Jesus to them. Eventually, what you breathe is the Lord Jesus, and what you speak is also the Lord Jesus. Then you will definitely be filled with the Triune God who is the Spirit.

I hope that you will start practicing in this way from today on. You should begin with calling on the Lord before getting out of bed, and then during the day, either call on the Lord or speak the Lord. As soon as you call on the Lord's name, the Spirit is with you; as soon as you speak the Lord's word, the Spirit will be with you even more. Romans 12:11 says that we have to be burning and hot in the spirit. When you call on the Lord as soon as you get up in the morning, you will be hot in your spirit. When you call a few more times, you will become burning in your spirit. If you will also speak the Lord Jesus, the Holy Spirit will fill you within. This is a very normal matter. This should be our normal daily living.

A message given by Brother Witness Lee in Taipei on October 13, 1987.

CHAPTER TEN

THE MIRACULOUS NORMALITY IN GOD'S ECONOMY

Scripture Reading: Rom. 10:6-13; 8:2, 6, 9-11

What I speak to you this morning may surprise you. However, if you have some deeper knowledge of the Bible and have experience in the spiritual life, you will know that what I am transfusing into you is accurate.

ALL THE MATTERS OF SPIRITUAL LIFE BEING NORMAL

Let me begin with my testimony. I was saved when I was nineteen years old. At that time, I was not clear regarding my salvation. Only afterward did I know that I was saved. At that time, I had a natural imagination within me that salvation should be an extraordinarily miraculous thing, and that some great things should happen to me. Although I did not express it, I had the concept that some extraordinary and unusual miracle should happen to me. Otherwise, how could I be considered saved? At that time, I pursued the Lord fervently. I read in the Bible that when the Holy Spirit came upon men, men began to speak in tongues (Acts 2:4; 10:45-46; 19:6). I then thought that if the Holy Spirit came upon me, I would also have some special manifestations. Some time later, I also read in Acts and the Epistles of Paul that the Holy Spirit wants to fill us within. I thought that this must also be an extraordinary thing. Therefore, I spent time to pursue the matters of experiencing salvation and the filling of the Holy Spirit. I pursued to the point of not sleeping or eating. I did not sleep well, nor did I have the desire to eat. I wanted to know whether I had actually been saved. However, no matter how much I tried, I did not obtain any extraordinary experience. Besides this, regarding being filled by the Spirit, I also pursued in a serious manner.

I was hoping that one day some great thing would happen to me. But after I had passed through many experiences, I had never had anything extraordinary happen to me. Instead, all that happened in my spiritual experience concerned merely normal matters. Today, over half a century has gone by. The more I have experienced, the more I feel that these matters of spiritual life, which are matters in God's New Testament economy, do not have anything that may shock people outwardly; rather, they all appear to be normal occurrences. When I first was saved, I was not clear concerning this point. But the more I experienced, the more I felt normal. And now, I see clearly that as far as spiritual matters are concerned, the more normal they are, the more proper and real they are. And the more normal they are, the more rich they are.

In the Bible there is a principle that the Lord uses the visible, tangible physical things to signify the invisible, intangible spiritual things. Every good Bible student admits this matter. God uses the tangible physical things in the universe to signify, represent, and describe the invisible spiritual things. In the past few decades, I have had several serious illnesses. I have discovered that our body is truly an organism full of the organic function. If you are ill, you do not depend only on taking medicine, but you must also depend on the organic function of the body itself. The human body is indeed wonderful. It is first conceived in the mother's womb; after development, the members of the body gradually become formed, and then the baby is born. During the development from a baby to a child, then to a young person, then to a middle-aged person, and then to an old person, many things take place. Yet these things that happen are altogether a matter of organic function. Every one of us is born with all the organic functions of our entire body; these functions are even the same in all of us. The organic functions of our physical life are real to us; in the same way, according to the revelation of the Bible, the life we obtained through regeneration is also real. This is not imagination or superstition. We can have this assurance, primarily not by our experience, but by the word of the Bible.

I can testify to you that the most valuable and superior book in the world is this Bible. If there were no God, human beings absolutely would not be able to write such a book. Throughout the generations, not one book of wisdom written by the philosophers could compare with the Bible. All the wonderful expressions, words of wisdom, and mysterious points in the Bible adequately prove the existence of God in the universe. They also prove that the spiritual life given by God is real. Moreover, from the viewpoint of experience, I can truly testify from more than sixty-three years' experience that the spiritual life of God within us is a reality. This is not the physical life created by God, but God coming into us, born within us, to be our life. Our outward man is the God-created life; our inward man is God being our life. Christianity has nearly discarded the aspect of God becoming our life within. They have also made the matter of the Holy Spirit coming upon men and the Holy Spirit filling men a rare and strange thing. In fact, this spiritual matter of God coming into us to be our life is a very normal matter. To be saved is a very normal matter. However, everyone who desires to be saved or who has been saved considers it as an extraordinary event and expects something unusual to happen to him when he is saved.

In 1938, I was preaching the gospel in my school in my home town. In the audience was a judge who also taught classes there; he became very interested as he listened. He came to me and said that he was willing to believe, but he did not know how to believe. I told him that he should simply kneel down beside his bed after he went home and pray to the Lord. After he went home, he did what I suggested. He told me afterward that while he was praying, he was preparing for something to happen to him. Although he waited quite a while, nothing happened. He thought that if believing in Jesus could cause one to be saved, then something had to happen. But why was nothing happening? He was afraid that what he had done did not work. Because he felt that his prayer did not work, he went to bed disappointed. The following morning, on the way to the courthouse, without any reason he suddenly sensed that the sky was beautiful, and the earth was also lovely. Formerly, whenever he saw a cat or a dog, he was disgusted. But now when he saw the dogs and cats running around on the street, he instead felt very interested in them. Whatever he saw, he felt it was lovely. After he went into the courthouse, his colleagues saw his face overflowing with smiles and asked him whether he had made a fortune, or why he was so happy. He could not tell how this had happened. While he was working, in his heart was happiness. After he went home from work, it was still like that. It was only after a few days that he realized that he was saved and that the Spirit of God had entered into him. At the time of his believing and prayer, nothing special had happened. It was in this way, however, that he was saved.

When I was a young person, eighteen or nineteen years old, what I liked the most was to play soccer and watch the Peking opera. Once I believed in the Lord, I did not do those two things again. Formerly, watching the Peking opera was really enjoyable, and playing soccer was really exciting. But after I was saved, although no one forbade me or taught me, I spontaneously lost my taste for those things. At that time, what I liked the best was reading the Bible, then prayer, and also preaching the gospel. I remember very well that at that time I loved reading the Bible to the point that the Bible never left my hands. When I lay in bed at night, I still would read a few more verses before turning off the lights. As soon as I woke up in the morning, even before I crawled out of the blankets, I took the Bible next to my pillow and began to read. No one had taught me; I simply loved reading the Bible, praying, and preaching the gospel. In the past sixty years, I have experienced a lot. The principle is the same. I have spoken all of these things with the intention of changing your natural concept that you may see that the matters of spiritual life are normal matters of spiritual life.

AN ILLUSTRATION FROM THE BIBLE

God's Salvation Having Been Prepared

Now I would use an illustration from the Bible to show you that matters of spiritual life are normal matters. Romans 10:6 says, "But the righteousness which is out of faith speaks in this way, Do not say in your heart, Who will ascend into heaven? That is, to bring Christ down." This portion of the word means that for our salvation, Christ needed to come down from heaven. But no one can ascend to heaven to bring Christ down. Furthermore, there was no need to bring Him down because He had already come down. Verse 7 then says, "Or, Who will descend into the abyss? That is, to bring Christ up from among the dead." The abyss is Hades. No one can cause Christ to come down from heaven, and then to descend to the abyss, and be resurrected from the dead. Christ has already accomplished all this for us. In other words, no one can do this thing; and neither is there any need for someone to do it, because Christ has already accomplished this for us. God has already prepared everything of His salvation for us. This can be compared to God preparing air for human beings on the earth, so that once a person is born, with a cry he can breathe the air into him. Today, if a person wants to be saved, he only needs to open his mouth and call, "O Lord Jesus!" Then he will obtain salvation.

Christ as the Word Being in Man's Mouth and in Man's Heart

Therefore, verse 8 continues, "But what does it say? The word is near you, in your mouth and in your heart." The "it" in this verse is "the righteousness" (in v. 6) which is "the word." This refers to Christ. This word of the Apostle Paul was spoken to those who had heard the gospel, but had not yet called on the Lord to be saved. After a person hears the gospel, before he calls on the Lord and believes, Christ is already in his mouth and in his heart. As soon as he calls, he will be saved.

When you go out to knock on doors to preach the gospel,

you should tell those who are listening to the gospel, "Christ is now in your mouth and in your heart." Although it is very difficult for people to comprehend this word, it is nevertheless a very normal matter because Christ has already accomplished everything, and through the word He has supplied everything. Today Christ is so wonderful that He is beyond our understanding. He has a person and a personality, but He is also like the air. This Christ is the righteousness of God to be our righteousness; hence, He needs to be received by us. For this, He needs to be the word, because only as the word are we able to hear and to receive Him. Once this Christ who is the word is heard by you, even though you have not yet believed in Him nor called on Him, He is already in your mouth and in your heart.

Therefore, you need to tell those who have heard the gospel and have not yet believed, "Friend, I am here to tell you some good news. You need the Savior. Although now you have not believed in Him yet, this Savior, along with the word of the gospel that you heard, has come into you already. As I am here speaking to you, He is in your mouth and in your heart. If you do not believe, the matter of salvation will still not be accomplished in you; however, as soon as you believe, the matter of salvation will be accomplished in you. This is just like the air being here. If you do not breathe, nothing will happen; as soon as you take a breath, the air comes into you. Today, for you to be saved is too simple a matter. There is no need to speak to the heavens and ask who will bring Christ down from heaven. Neither is there the need to speak to the earth and ask who will bring Christ up from beneath. The Christ that you need is now in your mouth and in your heart. You simply call on His name now! As soon as you call on His name, you will be saved. This is a very normal and easy matter."

The Reality of the Filling Being within Us and Accompanying Us Day by Day

It is also the same with the matter of being filled with

the Holy Spirit. The resurrected Christ as the reality of the filling of the Holy Spirit is within us, accompanying us day by day. The Lord's word says clearly, "I am with you all the days until the consummation of the age" (Matt. 28:20). The Lord accompanies us all the way; He is within us. Now you simply need to say, "Lord! Fill me!" You will be filled with the Holy Spirit. This is the secret of being filled with the Lord. You should never consider that being filled with the Holy Spirit is a very difficult matter, and that only those who have been saved over sixty years like me can have this experience. Let me tell you that even if you were saved today, you can be filled with the Holy Spirit. Every one of you can be filled with the Holy Spirit. I have been breathing for over eighty years. A newborn babe also breathes, and his breathing is the same as my breathing, with no difference at all.

Obtaining Salvation
by Confessing with the Mouth and
Believing in the Heart

Romans 10:9 says, "That if you confess with your mouth, Lord Jesus, and believe in your heart that God has raised Him from among the dead, you shall be saved." This word indicates that once a person has heard the gospel, he has in his mouth and in his heart the Savior who can save him. He only needs to confess Him as Lord with his mouth, that is, to open his mouth and call on His name, and he shall be saved. Verse 10 follows, saying, "For with the heart man believes unto righteousness, and with the mouth man confesses unto salvation." To confess with the mouth is to call on the Lord and also speak the Lord Jesus to others. Therefore, once a person is saved, you will need to lead him to speak the Lord Jesus to others, to speak to the parents, the wife, the husband, the children, and the neighbors. The more he speaks, the more he breathes. When we go to the communities to help people to be saved, we must set up home meetings in their homes so that they will not only call on the Lord's name, but also speak the Lord to others.

Enjoying the Lord's Riches
by Calling on His Name

Verses 11 and 12 continue, "For the Scripture says, All who believe on Him shall not be put to shame. For there is no difference between Jew and Greek; for the same Lord of all is rich to all who call upon Him." The secret of our enjoyment of all the riches of Christ is very simple. It is to call, "O Lord Jesus!" Calling on the Lord is really the secret of our enjoyment of all the riches of Christ. Therefore, for our salvation we need to call on Him; after salvation, daily, even hourly, we need to call on Him. Some will tell you that to be filled with the Holy Spirit, you need to fast, to confess, to empty yourself, to be broken, and also to pay the price to follow the Lord. When you hear this word, you may exercise much effort to fast and to pray. Eventually, you may obtain the filling. But actually, being filled with the Holy Spirit is not obtained by the act of fasting and praying; rather, it is obtained by the calling during the fasting and praying.

God as Our Life Having Become a Law

Romans chapter eight shows us that God coming into us to be our life is such a normal matter that it has become a law. The law of the Spirit of life has freed us and delivered us (v. 2). Every day we are breathing unceasingly; this is a law. The matter of God in us as our life is also a law; it is a very spontaneous matter. However, when the law of life is operating in us, we need to cooperate with it. Hence, verse 6 says, "For the mind set on the flesh is death, but the mind set on the spirit is life and peace." When we set our mind on the spirit to cooperate with the law of the Spirit of life, the issue is life and peace. The following verses from verse 9 to verse 11 mention God, Christ, and the Spirit at the same time. These three are one; this is simply the Triune God. Christ is within us; God is within us; and the Spirit is also within us. It is sufficient that we obey Him and cooperate with Him. This is the way to be filled with the Holy Spirit in our spirit.

TO BE ONE CALLING, ENJOYING, AND EXPERIENCING THE LORD REGULARLY AND IN A NORMAL WAY

According to my own experience, to be filled with the Spirit does not require much struggling or striving. You do not need to say, "Lord, I am too weak. I cannot help loving the world. I cannot free myself from my family affairs. I cannot drop my burdens. Lord, I can only be a fallen, backsliding Christian. Besides, I am no good in any-thing..." It is useless to pray this way. You need to realize that God in the economy of His spiritual life wants us to be those who call on the Lord, enjoy Him, and experience Him regularly and in a normal way.

Therefore, every morning when you get up, you should call, "O Lord Jesus!" to begin your spiritual breathing. You should call in this way all day long. Also, you cannot separate the word of the Lord from the Spirit of the Lord. Even the more, you cannot separate the Spirit of the Lord from the Lord Himself. The Lord is the Spirit, and the Spirit is the word. Not only did God come down to the earth from the heavens, and then from the earth to Hades; He also ascended to the heavens from Hades and became a life-giving Spirit. In the universe, among the human race, there is also the word of God written and printed here, and it has been left in our hands. Therefore, every morning as soon as we wake up, we need to call on Him and also receive His word. During the day, we simply do these two things: contact the Lord and receive His word. This is what is spoken of in *Hymns*, #501, stanza 4, which says:

> The Spirit of life causes Thee
> By Thy Word to transfer to me.
> Thy Spirit touched, Thy word received,
> Thy life in me is thus conceived.

We do not need much begging and groaning. I exhort you sisters who are housewives not to be bothered by your talkative husband, your troublesome children, and the endless household chores. All these are for the purpose of compelling you to call on the Lord. Today the Spirit is within us, and the Word is in our hands. All we need to do is to call on the Lord moment by moment and receive His word day by day. Then many of the problems will not exist. When we are weak, we feel that everything is difficult. When we are strong, however, we feel that nothing is difficult.

Brothers and sisters, the Lord as the Spirit is already in your mouth and in your heart. The Lord as the Word is also already in our hands and within us. Now you only need to receive the word and contact this Spirit, and the Lord will become your supply. Then day by day you will be saved and filled with the Holy Spirit, and you will allow the Holy Spirit to descend upon you. This should be your daily experience, which is normal, yet miraculous. Brother Moody once said, "The greatest miracle in the universe is that man can be regenerated." Truly, regeneration is a great thing in the universe. Every day in the spiritual life, we can experience this great thing in the universe. It is miraculous, yet normal. Therefore, it is a miraculous normality.

A message given by Brother Witness Lee in Taipei on October 15, 1987.

CHAPTER ELEVEN

PRACTICING SPEAKING THE LORD'S WORD WITH OUR SPIRIT

Scripture Reading: John 1:1; 6:63; 7:38; Rom. 10:8; Eph. 5:18-19; Col. 3:16-17

According to my observation, for the most part your meeting this morning has been like a theatrical performance. There has not been much content in the meeting. I hope that you will repent and be corrected from your heart. Those of you who have had meetings together with me can testify for me that in the past few decades, I have had the release of the spirit, pray-reading, and speaking in the meetings, but not once was there the flavor of a theatrical performance. As long as you have a little fun-making, a little jesting, that is a theatrical performance.

We need to see that regardless of where we are meeting, the basic element of our meeting is the worship of God. In John chapter four it is as if the Lord Jesus told the Samaritan woman, "I can give you living water. As long as you come to Me and drink of the water that I give you, you will never thirst again." That woman received this word and asked the Lord Jesus to give her the living water. The Lord Jesus said, "Go, call your husband and come here." What the Lord intended here was to guide her to confess and repent for the sin of adultery she had committed by marrying many husbands. Yet the woman replied, saying, "I don't have a husband." The Lord Jesus spoke to her gently, saying, "You have well said, I don't have a husband; for you have had five husbands, and the one you now have is not your husband." Once this immoral woman heard the Lord mentioning her disgraceful history, she changed the subject and started talking about the matter of worshipping God. She said, "Our fathers worshipped in this mountain, and you say that in

Jerusalem is the place where men must worship." The Lord
Jesus immediately corrected her, saying, "Neither in this
mountain nor in Jerusalem shall you worship the Father."
In discussing the matter concerning her husbands, the
Lord did not point out the sin of the woman directly;
rather, He commended her that she spoke well. But in
touching the matter of worshipping God, the Lord pointed
out her error. The Lord told her clearly that God is Spirit
and that man worships Him neither in this place nor in
that place, but in his spirit.

THE NEED FOR THE MEETING TO BE LIVING,
BUT NOT FUN-MAKING

I am speaking about this matter so that you may see
that even the matter of drinking the living water is
worship. The worship as revealed in the New Testament
and what has been passed on to us by Christianity are
absolutely different. The worship found in Christianity has
its origin in Catholicism, Catholic worship had its origin
in the degraded church, and in the matter of worship the
degraded church had fallen into pagan worship. But the
genuine worship of God as spoken of by the Lord is in
the spirit. Apparently, drinking the living water is not
worship, but actually this is the genuine worship. There is
no one, however, who drinks the living water on the one
hand, and performs and makes fun on the other. If you do
such a thing, it will definitely be impossible for the home
meetings and small group meetings to be built up, and the
changing of the system will definitely not be successful.
When the people who are proper see you making fun, they
will say, "I want Christ; I want the church. Even if I take
Christianity, I do not want this." You need to realize that
what subdues people is the spiritual reality. It is true that
when we come to the meetings, we do not want any
regulations or any of man's restrictions. We must, however,
avoid man's natural activities. There must not be any
intention to make fun. In the meetings, everyone should be
joyful, living, not restricted or bound, but not making fun
with one another according to the flesh. If you are living,

speaking to one another with the spirit, then when anyone, including the Devil, comes into the meeting, he will have to nod his head and say, "This group of people is truly worshipping before God, with no forms or regulations, and they are living to the uttermost, yet with no fun-making." Such a meeting is full of inspiration to move people and to give them a deep impression.

In these fifty or sixty years, I have had experiences of worshipping God. Once I see your improper behavior, I shake my head. I believe that most of the people cannot nod their heads either. As long as there are people making fun, the situation has to be corrected. Many times in the past, I have stood up in the meeting and corrected the situation, saying, "We cannot do things like this. This is playing, not worship." This is like what was spoken in Exodus, "The people sat down to eat and to drink, and rose up to play" (32:6). That was idol worship. We should not be making fun, but neither should we be restricted. We do not want restrictions, nor do we want fun-making. We are here in all propriety with our whole being—spirit, soul, and body—worshipping God in spirit. Particularly, we use our spirit through our mouth to release the Lord's word.

SPEAKING TO ONE ANOTHER WITH HYMNS

This morning, I would like you to see that our meetings, whether home meetings, small group meetings, or even large meetings, are a matter of speaking the Lord's word with the spirit. First Corinthians 14:26 says, "Whenever you come together, each one has a psalm...." In our mentality, once a psalm is mentioned, we think about singing. The New Testament, however, shows us that psalms are not primarily for singing, but for speaking. Ephesians 5:18-19 says, "Be filled in spirit, speaking to one another in psalms and hymns and spiritual songs, singing and psalming with your heart to the Lord." From this you can see that psalms are primarily for speaking, and then for singing. Also, Colossians 3:16, the sister verse to Ephesians 5:19, says the same thing, "Let the word of Christ dwell in you richly, in all wisdom teaching and

admonishing one another in psalms, hymns, and spiritual
songs, singing with grace in your hearts to God." It says
here that we should teach and admonish one another in
psalms, hymns, and spiritual songs. We have never
properly practiced this matter. We have been influenced
too deeply by Christianity. This time, regarding the matter
of meeting, we have to come back absolutely to the word of
the Bible—to teach and admonish one another in psalms.

For example, *Hymns*, #499, says:

> Oh, what a life! Oh, what a peace!
> The Christ who's all within me lives.
> With Him I have been crucified;
> This glorious fact to me He gives.
> Now it's no longer I that live,
> But Christ the Lord within me lives.

Suppose we have learned the way of not giving a
message, but speaking one to another with the contents of
the hymns. Which meeting do you think has greater
inspiration? It may be that we can try asking a brother to
speak a half-minute message according to this hymn, and
then have two other brothers speak to one another with
this hymn. Once you try this, you will know that speaking
to one another gives a strong inspiration and grants a deep
impression. The problem today is that in anything we do,
we cannot make it if we do not learn and practice. Even
inborn capabilities like the ability to walk still require
learning and practice. Therefore, the immediate need is to
have much practice and much learning after we have
changed the system.

First Corinthians 14:26 also says, "Each one has...a
teaching, has a revelation, has a tongue, has an interpretation. Let all things be done for building up." We have
already seen that hymns are not primarily for singing, but
for speaking. As far as "has a teaching" is concerned, of
course, it is a matter of speaking. "Has a revelation" is still
a matter of speaking. "Has a tongue, has an interpretation," needless to say, are also matters of speaking.
Every item is a matter of speaking.

BEING DESPERATE FOR THE CHANGE OF THE SYSTEM

Fifty years ago, our foremost brother, Watchman Nee, already saw that the Sunday service of Christianity is according to the customs of the nations and is not scriptural. He said that the Lord's Day message meeting is something of a waste, and that we should not consider this as the church meeting. After these messages were released, they were published in two books, *The Normal Christian Church Life* and *Church Affairs*, at two different times. At that time we saw that we should not maintain the Sunday morning meeting with one person speaking and the rest listening. However, we had no other way in our practice, because once we drop this practice of giving a message, there would be nothing else to replace it. Brother Nee and I talked about this matter and tried our best to find a way from the Bible, but eventually we did not find any way.

Although in 1984 we already had more than six hundred churches on the whole earth after these many years of experience, nevertheless the most important place in the Far East—Taipei—and the most important country in the West—the United States—were in a half-dormant state, with no spreading and no increase in number. For this I felt very bothered and also distressed. I felt I could not continue to carry out the outward spreading, even though there were people from many of the major cities of the six continents waiting to welcome me. I was even willing to sacrifice the work in the western world because I had to go back to Taiwan, which is the base of the Lord's recovery in the countries outside of mainland China, in order to resolve this problem. I am already more than eighty years old. I feel that I may not have too long a time on this earth. I do not desire to be looking at such a situation and cheerlessly leave this world. I also know that for me to come to Taiwan to work in this way is risking my life. Moreover, such a great task and heavy burden should not be pressing upon me. But I feel that I am bound by this duty. I have told the brothers here a number of times that I will labor until my death. Within the limits the Lord has given me, I have assigned the co-workers. I have moved nearly all the useful ones here, whether Chinese or foreign. The Lord has also confirmed this matter. The churches, especially those in the United States, responded to this immediately and offered abundantly for this cause. The reason that we have mobilized our manpower and finances to such a great extent to study and carry out this matter is that, based on decades of experience, we feel this matter is not easy to change; yet it has to be changed. Until now, we have spent three full years of time; thank the Lord, we have already obtained a very good result.

SPEAKING THE LORD'S WORD WITH THE SPIRIT AND FLOWING OUT RIVERS OF LIVING WATER

In this morning's training meeting, I would like to fellowship these matters with you clearly. You need to realize that the genuine Christian meeting according to God's New Testament economy is one where every believer uses the spirit to speak the Lord's word as soon as he arrives at the meeting. You may say that this matter has been tested successfully in our training laboratory. Now we must carry out this matter among the brothers and sisters. This requires that all of us be diligent to lead them and teach them.

John 1:1 says that in the beginning was the Word, and the Word was God, who is the Triune God. Chapter six, verse 63, continues to say that the word the Lord speaks to us is spirit. Therefore, the Word is God, and the Word is also the Spirit. Then 7:38 says that once we believe in the Lord, we receive the Spirit; the result is that there are rivers of living water flowing out of us. The rivers of living water are the Lord's words that are flowing out unceasingly. These three portions of the Scriptures show us that the Triune God as the Word becomes the Spirit to enter into us. When we speak the Lord's word with the Spirit, He will flow out from within us. Moreover, since the Triune God is the Word, Romans 10:8 says that this word is near us, in our mouth and in our heart.

This is a very weighty and real fact. Nevertheless, our realization is not adequate. We still think that God is great, holy, and lofty; how could He be with us in such a simple way? Actually, to us the Triune God is just like air, being with us in every place at every time, although we are not conscious of Him. This is a miraculous normality. It is very miraculous, yet very normal. For God to be with us is extremely simple; He is in our mouth and in our heart.

Since this is a fact, then we should be filled in spirit with the Triune God, as recorded in Ephesians 5:18, so that out from within us can flow rivers of living water. How do these rivers of living water flow out? This is through the speaking to one another as mentioned in verse 19. With what should we speak to one another? With psalms, hymns, and spiritual songs. Throughout the years many experienced ones among us have spent a lot of effort to compile many psalms and spiritual songs. These are printed in our hymnal and are ready to be used, without the need at any time for us to compile or to consider. For example, *Hymns*, #501, says:

> O glorious Christ, Savior mine,
> Thou art truly radiance divine;
> God infinite, in eternity,
> Yet man in time, finite to be.
>
>> Oh! Christ, expression of God, the Great,
>> Inexhaustible, rich, and sweet!
>> God mingled with humanity
>> Lives in me my all to be.

You can see that these words are so brief, yet to the point. You can say that every word is golden. None of us is able to utter such a word. However, now we only need to open up the hymnal to speak and read to one another just like the way we use the Bible. In this way through our speaking with the spirit, the Triune God who fills us within will flow out like rivers of living water.

I have already pointed out that Ephesians 5:18-19 and Colossians 3:16 are sister portions. Ephesians speaks concerning being filled with the Spirit, and Colossians speaks concerning being filled with the word. These two are one thing. When these portions of Scripture are put together, they prove to us that our speaking the Lord's word with the spirit is to flow out the Holy Spirit. The word and the Spirit are one. For this reason, every one of us, especially the trainees, from now on should have much practice to speak the Lord's word with the spirit just as we would practice calligraphy or piano. Once you enter into the meeting, regardless of whether it is a home meeting, a small group meeting, or a large meeting, you need to open your mouth and speak the Lord's word with the Spirit. When a brother comes to the meeting, suppose he opens his mouth and says, "Praise the Lord! John 1:1 says, 'In the beginning was the Word, and the Word was with God, and the Word was God.'" Another sister may follow and say, "In the beginning, in the beginning, was the Word...." There is no need to have a person find a particular topic to speak to the others. Every portion of the Scripture is usable because all Scripture is God-breathed. Every chapter is the Lord's word; every verse is life. Someone may select Matthew 1:1, saying, "The book of the generation of Jesus Christ, Son of David, Son of Abraham." Every one should be living, and every one should speak the Lord's word in the meetings. From now on, we all need to exercise to speak the Lord's word with the spirit. We may use the Bible to speak, or we may use a hymn to speak. It is not too difficult to do this well, as long as everyone is willing to practice sincerely.

Sometimes we may feel the need to learn some truths; then we may use the *Life Lessons* or the *Truth Lessons*. But there should not be one person speaking and the rest listening. It is necessary for every one to practice releasing the spirit, speaking the Lord's word to one another. You need to realize that after we have changed the system, our responsibility will be very heavy. It will still be necessary for the main part of the brothers and sisters of every meeting hall and district to take the lead to speak the Lord's word with the Spirit, and also to do their best to lead others to practice. In this way, our meetings will become living and will be able to entirely replace the meetings of one person speaking with the rest listening.

A message given by Brother Witness Lee in Taipei on October 20, 1987.

CHAPTER TWELVE

THE ISSUES AND MANIFESTATIONS
OF THE FILLING AND THE OUTPOURING
OF THE SPIRIT

Scripture Reading: Acts 13:52; Eph. 5:18-19; Col. 3:16; 1 Cor. 12:7-8, 10; Rom. 8:4; Gal. 5:16, 25, 22-23; Acts 2:4; 10:45-46; 19:6; 1 Cor. 12:9-10; Acts 4:8, 31; 13:9

We need to continue what we have studied and emphasized here in the past and see together the secrets of building up the home meetings. We have pointed out that the crucial elements of meeting are the word, the Spirit, singing, and praying. If you want the meetings to be living and rich, they need to be full of the Lord's word, and the word must have the Spirit. If the word does not have the spirit, then it is merely the letter; it is dead and empty, and it causes people to be depressed. The word of God must have the Spirit in order to be life. Therefore, fundamentally, Christian meetings should be full of the word of God, and the word of God should be filled with the mingled Spirit of God. When we come to the meeting, the first thing is to sing the word of God with the spirit. The second thing is to pray, and there should be much prayer. Regardless of whether we are in the home meetings, small group meetings, district meetings, or even in large meetings, we have to practice these four things: the word, the Spirit, singing, and praying. After praying, you have to speak; after speaking, you have to sing; after singing, you still have to pray. In this way, our meetings will definitely be living, high, rich, and full of impact.

THE MEETINGS AS AN ISSUE AND AN EXPRESSION
OF OUR LIVING

In the recent past, we have conducted some experiments to practice these four things in different kinds of meetings. However, the results have not been entirely satisfactory.

Our situation is still too rigid and monotonous. Therefore, I spent time to study again all twenty-seven books of the New Testament, from Matthew to Revelation, to have a reconsideration. When I put together all the verses concerning meeting, I can see that the meeting of the believers is not an independent matter, but an issue and expression of our daily living. How we have our daily living will determine how we meet when we come together. If our daily living is of one condition, yet we come to the meeting and put on masks like those in the opera to portray something of another condition, that is not a meeting, but a performance. Our Christian meetings must be genuine; the more genuine they are, the more proper they are. How we are in our daily life should be how we are in the meetings. We must be genuine, without any falsehood at all. It should not be that you do not talk in your daily life, yet you talk without stopping in the meetings. Neither should it be that you talk so roughly in your daily living, yet you speak so gently when you are in the meetings. When the Lord Jesus was on earth, He rebuked the Pharisees as hypocrites. At that time, this word hypocrites was used to refer to the Greek and Roman actors who spoke wearing a mask; hence, they were false and were pretending. Our Christian meetings should not be like that.

CHRISTIAN LIVING AND MEETING
BEING OF THE SPIRIT

Therefore our meeting cannot be separated from our daily living. The entire New Testament reveals to us that Christian living is not a matter of teaching and doctrine, but a matter of the Spirit. The verses we quoted this morning show us that Christian living is a living of being filled with the Spirit. Ephesians is a profound book. At the end it says, "Do not be drunk with wine... but be filled in spirit" (5:18). According to the entire revelation of the book of Ephesians, to be filled in spirit is to be filled with the Triune God. Today our God has passed through many processes, and He has been prepared. This processed Triune God has become the all-inclusive Spirit. He is just like the air, upon us, in our mouth, and even within us. Simply by taking a breath, we can be filled with Him. Eventually, we will be "speaking to one another in psalms and hymns and spiritual songs." From this you can see that the living of the members of the Body of Christ must be filled in spirit with the Triune God. Romans chapter eight also has a similar word telling us that the genuine spirituality is to walk not according to the flesh, but according to the spirit (v. 4). Galatians chapter five also says that we who live by the Spirit should also walk by the Spirit (v. 25). These words adequately prove that Christian living is altogether a matter of the Spirit.

If we have this kind of living, when we come together, we will also have this kind of meeting. Our living is of the Spirit; our meeting is also of the Spirit. This is altogether a matter in the Spirit. If we merely have the Spirit, yet we are not in the spirit, then our living is not a Christian living; rather, it is no different from that of the worldly people. In that case, when we come together, of course, there would be no Christian meeting. In the worldly meetings, people are gathered together, and each one is seated in an orderly way one by one. There may be someone in the meeting making an announcement on a specific matter, or someone giving a speech. When we Christians are not in the spirit, our meetings will also be like this. The ushers will invite everyone to be seated. When the time comes, an elder will call a hymn, another elder will offer a prayer, and then a brother who does the speaking will give a message. If he speaks well, everybody will be happy; if he does not speak well, everyone will be disappointed. If the speaking is good, everyone will offer some praise; if the speaking is not good, some will criticize him behind his back and will not even want to come back again. This kind of meeting can sometimes offer people some edification. But as a whole, it does not perfect people, nor does it edify the spirits of the Christians. It does not build up together the members of the Body of Christ in the Spirit of Christ.

In order to have the God-ordained meetings according to the New Testament economy as revealed in the Bible, the persons attending the meetings must be living in their daily life, overcoming, not loving the world, not lusting after sin, not living by the flesh, and not pitying the self. Also, they need to exercise their spirit to call on the Lord Jesus moment by moment, fellowship with the Lord unceasingly, and speak the Lord's word to others all the time. This is the daily life we ought to have. Unfortunately, many among us lack this kind of exercise. When they get up in the morning, they do not call on the Lord's name. Naturally, they do not have prayer or the reading of the Word. They are merely busy with different matters all day long. All six days of the week they do not live in the spirit, nor do they fellowship with the Lord. Of course, their heart toward the Lord becomes cold. And gradually, they fall into the world, live according to the flesh, and even fall into the snares of sin. When the Lord's Day comes, because they are believers, they cannot stay away and not come to even one meeting a week; therefore, they come to the meeting. However, though their body has come to the meeting, they are dead inside. Even if they want to say something, they do not know what to say. They may want to call out, yet they cannot; they simply have to sit there in silence. Under such a situation, there is, of course, the need for someone to come to give a message. In today's Christianity, whether Catholicism or Protestantism, and even among us, the general situation of the meeting is like this. This is not a meeting of the living, but a meeting of the dead. The large meeting is a meeting of the dead; the small meeting is also a meeting of the dead. If this is the case, even if the church changes the system, it will be useless.

Therefore, in studying the Lord's new way, we have discovered in the end that this is a key issue. If we cannot have a breakthrough on this point, by the Lord's mercy, regardless of what kind of change we have in our ways, it will be useless. That would be just like changing the coffin for the dead. If the large meetings are changed to small meetings, and one person speaking is changed to many persons speaking, yet the people still are not living, not able to utter a word, then we might as well take the old way to invite a pastor or a preacher to come to give a message, so that at least he may have something to say. This would still be better than changing to small meetings where you look at me and I look at you, yet with no one able to utter anything. Therefore, I advise you that if everyone is not living, not in the spirit, then we do not want to change the system.

RECOVERING THE NEW TESTAMENT MEETING

Our foremost brother, Watchman Nee, who brought the Lord's recovery to us, pointed out quite early in his messages that the Lord's Day morning message meeting is according to the customs of the nations; it is a waste, and we do not need to maintain it. Fifty years ago, not only did I hear him say this, but I also discussed with him how to eliminate the Lord's Day message meeting. I still remember him saying that 1 Corinthians 14:26 tells us clearly that when the whole church gathers together, it is not one person speaking and the rest listening, but each one has a hymn, or has a revelation, or has a teaching. It is evident that the meeting is mutual, with one another, and is not one-sided. We must return to such a situation. Later on, we decided to gather the brothers together to practice first. When these brothers came together, we absolutely did not want anyone to take the lead, or any one person to select the hymns, or pray, or give a message. Everyone could open his mouth to pray, to speak, to testify, or to call a hymn. This was the brothers' meeting at that time. At the beginning, this one testified, and that one also testified. But after two or three months, the testimonies were exhausted, and there was nothing else to do. Hence, that trial was not successful. Afterwards, we came to Taiwan. We still tried our best to have brothers' meetings and sisters' meetings in Taipei. However, before long they had to stop those meetings due to the lack of speaking. At the beginning Brother Nee had already said that in order to eliminate the Lord's Day message meeting, there was the need of a better substitute. Otherwise, we can predict already that as soon as the meeting with one person speaking and the rest listening is eliminated, a small number among us who like to listen to messages may go to other places to listen to messages. Needless to say, those outsiders who like to listen to messages and attend services will not come either.

THE KEY TO THE SUCCESS
OF THE CHANGE OF THE SYSTEM

I would like to let all of you know that what we have done recently to change the system may be considered a success in every respect. Regarding the matter of preaching the gospel by visiting peoples' homes, as long as you would do this according to the secrets we have discovered through our study, you will definitely gain people. Not only has this matter been tested successfully here in Taipei, but among the churches on the six continents of the earth, many places have also tested it successfully. Now the key is how to bring the brothers and sisters into the spirit to live and walk by the Spirit daily and to become overcomers. If there are ten persons meeting, and four or five among them are like this, then there will be no problem with that meeting. Of course, we hope that every brother and sister will live in the spirit, but church history has shown us that probably only on the day of Pentecost were every one of the hundred and twenty disciples and the three thousand newly saved ones filled with the Spirit. After that, even at Paul's time, the meetings of the saints also had imperfect areas. Some walked by the Spirit, and some did not walk by the Spirit. Therefore, after much study, we expect to have only twenty-five percent. What this means is that if we went out to knock on doors to preach the gospel and baptized one thousand people, we would expect only two hundred fifty to stand firm. And among these two hundred fifty, we would expect only about sixty to be used by the Lord. Based on this way of budgeting, if in a meeting of ten people there are two or three persons who are living, then we will consider that as successful. According to this standard, our change of the system will surely succeed. Of course, the key to this success still lies in our endeavoring.

THE ISSUES AND MANIFESTATIONS OF THE FILLING
AND OUTPOURING OF THE HOLY SPIRIT

The New Testament shows us that concerning the issues and manifestations of the filling and outpouring of the Spirit, only a small number of items are miraculous, such as tongue-speaking, healing, works of power, and predicting. In Paul's Epistles, he did not encourage people to exercise these four kinds of gifts in the meeting. On the contrary, he said in 1 Corinthians chapter fourteen that if there is one who wants to speak in tongues in the meeting, but there is no one to interpret, then that one should be silent (vv. 27-28). We cannot find any evidence from the Bible that there definitely should be the works of power, tongue-speaking, healing, or predicting in the meetings. Therefore, we should not be disturbed by thinking that these few items must be in the meetings. What the Bible considers to be the more important issues and manifestations of the filling and outpouring of the Spirit are five items in the essential (filling) aspect:

The first is being filled with joy and the Holy Spirit (Acts 13:52). Whether you feel troubled or sorrowful, you only need to call, "O Lord Jesus!" You will become joyful and be filled with the Holy Spirit.

The second is speaking words of praise, of teaching, and of admonition (Eph. 5:18-19; Col. 3:16). These words are already in the Bible, which is the "word of Christ" mentioned in Colossians chapter three. The psalms, hymns, and spiritual songs mentioned in Ephesians chapter five are not only in the Bible, but also in our hymnal. For example, *Hymns*, #501, says:

> O glorious Christ, Savior mine,
> Thou art truly radiance divine;
> God infinite, in eternity,
> Yet man in time, finite to be.
>
> Oh! Christ, expression of God, the Great,
> Inexhaustible, rich, and sweet!
> God mingled with humanity
> Lives in me my all to be.

These well-speakings are really too good! If you cannot recite the hymns, at least you should learn to memorize what each hymn talks about. Concerning the Bible, you should at least remember what each book and each chapter talks about. For example, the first section of Matthew 5 talks about the nine blessings given by the Lord Jesus. When you come to the meeting, if you have the inspiration within, you may tell everyone, "Let us turn to Matthew 5:3." Immediately after you find that page, you may say, "Blessed are the poor in spirit." There should be someone to continue spontaneously by saying, "for theirs is the kingdom of the heavens." When you read these nine blessings in a living way with some declarations, everyone will receive the edification. We all need to practice this. First practice in your home, using the words of the Bible or the hymns to speak one to another. When you go to the small group meeting, use these words to speak to others. In this way, the entire meeting will become living. We all need to practice speaking these two kinds of words; one kind are the words from the Bible, and the other kind are the words of the hymns.

The third is speaking the word of wisdom, the word of knowledge, and the word of prophecy (1 Cor. 12:7-8, 10). This is to speak the revelation concerning God and Christ, speaking for God and speaking forth God.

The fourth is living by the Spirit and walking according to the Spirit (Rom. 8:4; Gal. 5:16, 25). As soon as we get up every morning, we should call, "O Lord Jesus!" We should practice this all day long, and gradually we will live according to the Spirit. This is also what it means to be filled with the Spirit.

Fifth, when we live by the Spirit and walk according to the Spirit, the result is that we will be able to bear the fruit of the Spirit (Gal. 5:22-23). If we live in this way, we will surely desire to meet together. Moreover, regardless of whether we meet with family members, or with a small number of saints, or even with many saints, our meetings will definitely be living and rich.

Then, in the economical (pouring out) aspect, besides

tongue-speaking, predicting, healing, and works of power (Acts 2:4; 10:45-46; 19:6; 1 Cor. 12:9-10), the most important item is to speak the word of God with boldness (Acts 4:8, 31; 13:9). As long as we live by the Spirit, walk according to the Spirit, and are overcomers, when we come to the meeting, spontaneously we will speak the word of God and testify for the Lord with boldness. These are the issues and manifestations of the filling and the outpouring of the Spirit.

A message given by Brother Witness Lee in Taipei on October 22, 1987.